MOBILE SOCIAL MARKETING IN LIBRARIES

Library Technology Essentials

About the Series

The *Library Technology Essentials* series helps librarians utilize today's hottest new technologies as well as ready themselves for tomorrow's. The series features titles that cover the A–Z of how to leverage the latest and most cutting-edge technologies and trends to deliver new library services.

Today's forward-thinking libraries are responding to changes in information consumption, new technological advancements, and growing user expectations by devising groundbreaking ways to remain relevant in a rapidly changing digital world. This collection of primers guides libraries along the path to innovation through step-by-step instruction. Written by the field's top experts, these handbooks serve as the ultimate gateway to the newest and most promising emerging technology trends. Filled with practical advice and projects for libraries to implement right now, these books inspire readers to start leveraging these new techniques and tools today.

About the Series Editor

Ellyssa Kroski is the Director of Information Technology at the New York Law Institute as well as an award-winning editor and author of 22 books including *Law Librarianship in the Digital Age* for which she won the AALL's 2014 Joseph L. Andrews Legal Literature Award. Her ten-book technology series, The Tech Set, won the ALA's Best Book in Library Literature Award in 2011. She is a librarian, an adjunct faculty member at Pratt Institute, and an international conference speaker. She speaks at several conferences a year, mainly about new tech trends, digital strategy, and libraries.

Titles in the Series

1. *Wearable Technology: Smart Watches to Google Glass for Libraries*, by Tom Bruno
2. *MOOCs and Libraries*, by Kyle K. Courtney
3. *Free Technology for Libraries*, by Amy Deschenes
4. *Makerspaces in Libraries*, by Theresa Willingham and Jeroen De Boer
5. *Knowledge Management for Libraries*, by Valerie Forrestal
6. *WordPress for Libraries*, by Chad Haefele
7. *Game It Up! Using Gamification to Incentivize Your Library*, by David Folmar
8. *Data Visualizations and Infographics*, by Sarah K. C. Mauldin
9. *Mobile Social Marketing in Libraries*, by Samantha C. Helmick
10. *Digital Collections and Exhibits*, by Juan Denzer
11. *Using Tablets and Apps in Libraries*, by Elizabeth Willse
12. *Responsive Web Design in Practice*, by Jason A. Clark

MOBILE SOCIAL MARKETING IN LIBRARIES

Samantha C. Helmick

ROWMAN & LITTLEFIELD
Lanham • Boulder • New York • London

Published by Rowman & Littlefield
A wholly owned subsidiary of The Rowman & Littlefield Publishing Group, Inc.
4501 Forbes Boulevard, Suite 200, Lanham, Maryland 20706
www.rowman.com

Unit A, Whitacre Mews, 26-34 Stannary Street, London SE11 4AB

British Library Cataloguing in Publication Information Available

Library of Congress Cataloging-in-Publication Data

Helmick, Samantha C., 1985–
Mobile social marketing in libraries / Samantha C. Helmick.
pages cm. – (Library technology essentials ; 9)
Includes bibliographical references and index.
ISBN 978-1-4422-4380-4 (cloth : alk. paper) – ISBN 978-1-4422-4381-1 (pbk. : alk. paper) – ISBN 978-1-4422-4382-8 (ebook)
1. Libraries–Marketing. 2. Online social networks–Library applications. I. Title.
Z716.3.H43 2015
302.30285–dc23
2015013853

∞ ™ The paper used in this publication meets the minimum requirements of American National Standard for Information Sciences Permanence of Paper for Printed Library Materials, ANSI/NISO Z39.48-1992.

Printed in the United States of America

CONTENTS

SERIES EDITOR'S FOREWORD

The social networking hubs of just a few years ago have been amplified or replaced by mobile apps that enable communication and connections on the go. *Mobile Social Marketing in Libraries* explains how to use today's most popular mobile social networking apps to reach out to library patrons, promote your library, and build community. Mobile social guru Samantha Helmick has written an essential guidebook that illustrates how to create an effective library presence within these well-attended communities from project ideas and planning to marketing and best practices. From start to finish, readers will learn how to create interactive, teen-friendly Tumblrs, how to use Snapchat for social media marketing, how to offer reader's advisory with Instagram, and how to create Vines for library instruction.

The idea for the Library Technology Essentials book series came about because there have been many drastic changes in information consumption, new technological advancements, and growing user expectations over the past few years, which forward-thinking libraries are responding to by devising groundbreaking ways to remain relevant in a rapidly changing digital world. I saw a need for a practical set of guidebooks that libraries could use to inform themselves about how to stay on the cutting edge by implementing new programs, services, and technologies to match their patrons' expectations.

Libraries today are embracing new and emerging technologies, transforming themselves into community hubs and places of cocreation through makerspaces, developing information common spaces, and even taking on new roles and formats, all the while searching for ways to decrease budget lines, add value, and prove the ROI (return on investment) of the library. The Library Technology Essentials series is a collection of primers to guide libraries along the path to innovation through step-by-step instruction. Written by the field's top experts, these handbooks are meant to serve as the ultimate gateway to the newest and most promising emerging technology trends. Filled with practical advice and project ideas for libraries to implement right now, these books will hopefully inspire readers to start leveraging these new techniques and tools today.

Each book follows the same format and outline, guiding the reader through the A–Z of how to leverage the latest and most cutting-edge technologies and trends to deliver new library services. The "projects" chapter comprises the largest portion of the books, providing library initiatives that can be implemented by both beginner and advanced readers, accommodating for all audiences and levels of technical expertise. These projects and programs range from the basic "How to Circulate Wearable Technology in Your Library" and "How to Host a FIRST Robotics Team at the Library" to intermediate, such as "How to Create a Hands-Free Digital Exhibit Showcase with Microsoft Kinect" to the more advanced options, such as "Implementing a Scalable E-Resources Management System" and "How to Gamify Library Orientation for Patrons with a Top-Down Video Game." These projects and programs range from procedural marketing techniques like "How to Create a Facebook Group for a Library Book Club" and "How to Use Snapchat for Library Social Media Marketing," to specific mobile social media marketing objectives such as "How to Use Vine for Library Instruction," and "How to Provide Reader's Advisory through Instagram." Readers of all skill levels will find something of interest in these books.

Samantha Helmick has been writing and speaking about outreach and social media marketing in libraries for years as well as serving as the social media face of her library in her position as UX (user experience) and outreach librarian at the Burlington Public Library (Iowa). I knew that if anyone was qualified to write a top-notch, cutting-edge book on mobile social marketing in libraries it was Sam. And she did just that. Samantha is one of those professionals who just "gets it," and she has filled this exceptional book with sage advice and exciting program ideas.

If you want to learn all the ins and outs of mobile social marketing for your library, this is the book for you.

Ellyssa Kroski
Director of Information Technology
The New York Law Institute
http://www.ellyssakroski.com
http://ccgclibraries.com
ellyssakroski@yahoo.com

PREFACE

Ten years ago, libraries reconciled with the importance of their web presence. Users flocked to many library sites to discover patched work spanning various content providers or sites strong in content yet lacking in design. A surge of web and mobile design advocates and tools hit the field of library and information science. Library schools began to require coding and digital design in their coursework. Small and large libraries grappled to define their digital presence as budgets were allocated and new staff were hired to manifest the library as a physical space and also now a mobile space.

Today, librarians recognize the importance of clear, accessible online domains to attract and serve users. However, as users migrate from websites to mobile applications the rising issue becomes the formation of a library's presence on mobile social media. Contemporary professionals are challenged with a similar task librarians faced a decade ago: finding users where they spend their time and maintaining a strong marketing relationship with users in their digital domain. As the consumption of mobile social technology increases, librarians are afforded the opportunity to stay ahead of the trend and to teach their users the principles of mobile social network use.

Mobile Social Marketing in Libraries is an examination of popular mobile social platforms, in particular, and their usefulness as marketing tools for libraries. Each moment of the day, millions upon millions of messages connect citizens of the digital world through various networks. Snapchat boasts four hundred million users. Instagram has more than 130 million users. Vine is brimming with forty million users, and Tumblr keeps growing past 126 million users. With strategic planning, libraries could harness the popularity of these social spaces and apply appropriate marketing schemes to each network in order to gain awareness and increase library use.

Mobile social marketing networks have leveled the playing field for advertising by providing relatively easy-to-use structures for communication. Both urban and rural users, from all walks of life, can be connected through mobile social platforms within their living rooms or on the go. Libraries the world over can find and engage with their service community members with just a few taps of an application.

Discover how to leverage the popularity of new mobile social applications for library marketing by joining these social networks and creating engaging content. Learn how to encourage library patrons to create their own content and tag it with the library's location. Successfully advertise a new series of programs, promote traditional resources, and place a hand on the pulse of the library's service community with steps included in these chapters.

This practical handbook will walk readers through the process of planning, creating, and sharing mobile social marketing content for your library. The following book offers insight into the essentials of using mobile social marketing apps in the context of library engagement.

The early chapters on this book lay out the principal networks used for marketing by corporations, organizations, and community groups. Case studies in chapter 4 will offer insight into how libraries are already using mobile social networks to communicate with users and tell their library's story. Read examples of libraries using mobile social marketing applications to enhance the library experience. From the City of London's Guildhall Library celebrating the 450th anniversary of Shakespeare's birthday on Twitter to the Oskaloosa Library in Iowa sharing popular content on its Teen Zone Tumblr page, the creative use of mobile social marketing will be explored.

The step-by-step projects in chapter 5 will lead the reader through the ins and outs of how best to leverage each mobile social network (Instagram, Snapchat, Tumblr, and Vine, as well as Twitter and Facebook) for library marketing, instruction, outreach, and other services. Readers are given a guide to use in the creation of long-term library campaigns, mobile reference, and marketing strategies for their own libraries. Additional tips and tricks to personalize mobile social marketing will be explained in chapter 6 along with the extrapolation of third-party apps for each network. Future trends for mobile social marketing as well as useful resources for ongoing skill development are discussed in chapter 7. The book finalizes with a chapter dedicated to providing additional resources to explore.

Upon completing this book, readers will feel confident in the direction of their library's mobile social marketing strategy and well equipped to create and maintain marketing strategies through various mobile social marketing platforms.

ACKNOWLEDGMENTS

I would like to express my gratitude to many people who saw me through this book; to friends who provided support, colleagues who allowed me to quote their remarks, and my editor, Ellyssa, for her brilliantly innovative outlook and genuine enthusiasm to share knowledge.

I would like to thank you for reading this book as you endeavor to expand your skill sets and provide quality mobile engagement. Above all I want to thank my parents, Dawn, Raleigh, and Nancy, who never fail to challenge, encourage, and inspire.

1

AN INTRODUCTION TO MOBILE SOCIAL MARKETING

Mobile social marketing is more than the capability to remotely sell a brand while wearing pajamas. The mobile social marketing approach answers various needs for libraries from same-time reference and increased outreach and promotion to digital advancement. As user needs change and budgets crunch, libraries are left to meet the new opportunities of digital engagement and technology instruction.

WHAT ARE MOBILE SOCIAL MARKETING APPLICATIONS?

To understand what a mobile social marketing application encompasses and accomplishes, the definition of a social network must be examined. A social network is a collection of people bound together through a specific set of social relations that permits the exchange of information. While a social network can be a family, group of friends, or a gathering of colleagues, for the purpose of this conversation, a social network is defined as a self-managed matrix allowing participants to create personal connections directly while others support community-based groups with aligned interests.

Examples of social networks that have adopted mobile applications for expanded mobile use are Twitter, Facebook, and Tumblr. Other social applications such as Instagram and Snapchat were born in the mobile world and solely exist as mobile networks. Common characteristics of all mobile social networks include access to information and the ability to share that information textually and graphically.

The benefits of marketing through mobile social applications include:

- Quick and easy transition for users to move from off-line to online content
- Opportunity for powerful, engaging, interactive experiences
- Increased response rates and captured qualified leads
- Measurable metrics for marketing, advertising, promotion, and social media campaigns

Quick and Easy Transition for Users to Move from Off-line to Online Content

Mobile social applications have enabled libraries to connect users with digital content. Imagine the ease with which a link to a catalog search, database, or e-resource can be applied to transactions on the library's Facebook or Twitter account. Mobile social applications permit a direct relationship between introducing a library's digital content and enabling a user to explore the content instantaneously.

Employing Vine to create a preliminary, graphic summary of a library's e-book consortium or language learning software and then applying access links to the video description is a relatively simple method of offering a quick and clarion transition for library users toward online content.

Opportunity for Powerful, Engaging, Interactive Experiences

The power behind an invigorating reference transaction or reader's advisory exchange can at times be unparalleled. However, dialogue expressed through mobile social applications can be premeditated to enhance the appeal to library users.

Compared to library advertising through traditional methods such as radio promotion or through the local newspaper, advertising through mobile social applications invites users to respond. When the library's summer reading program is announced on the radio or a student orientation event is published in the college newspaper, users are asked to apply the information given and determine a course of action. When these events are publicized through mobile social networks, the language applied can be less formal and limited, users can immediately request additional information, and the possibility of unassociated engagement exists.

Increased Response Rates and Captured Qualified Leads

An instance of possibility for unassociated engagement is formed by simply asking a question by way of announcing an upcoming event, new material, or available resource: "Summer Reading begins June 6th. Are you ready?" Responses to a library's attempts of associated or unassociated engagement can be qualified and observed to gain insight into the behavior of potential library users.

In the marketing profession, people who show the intent and ability to make a purchase decision within a reasonable time frame are referred to as qualified leads. The audience of a library's mobile social network are composed of leads from non-library users and current participants with the potential to utilize the library in varied ways. Increasingly, libraries are quantifying response and capturing qualified leads to follow through their utility model in regard to reference, circulation, and programming services.

Analytics follow predictable patterns in many instances. Content marketers have used data from library user responses to determine that posts or mobile social application updates are most successfully received during peak days and times. Facebook content receives the majority of its reach when posted on Thursdays from 9:00 a.m. to noon. Tweets are viewed by more followers when they are submitted on Fridays between 2:00 p.m. and 3:00 p.m. In the same vein of predictability, qualified leads for reference services increase during midterms and finals, while children's programming leads increase during the summer months.

The challenge to librarians is to ascertain ongoing qualified leads, which may not be as evident as other calls for service and marketing of such services, and to grow unique unassociated engagement opportunities in order to capture qualified leads from library users and potential library users. Information gleaned from interactions made possible through mobile social applications can assist librarians in the formation of richer dialogue and marketing in the future.

Measurable Metrics for Marketing, Advertising, Promotion, and Social Media Campaigns

An advantage of mobile social application marketing for libraries is the capacity to measure the reach of library marketing, promotion, and media campaigns. Before mobile social applications made it possible for an audience to respond and interact with advertising, libraries depended predominantly on word-of-mouth feedback and participation figures to determine the outcome of their promotion and media campaigns.

Today, word-of-mouth feedback and participation figures are vital and have been complemented with new data measuring the impact of library marketing. Social networks like Facebook and Twitter send weekly administrative updates to users managing social profiles. Facebook tracks several different statistics, such as new "likes" and the number of visitors. Developers offer an array of third-party applications that allow users to track new followers, unfollowers, retweets, mentions, tags, and responses.

Quick access to mobile social application statistics teaches librarians which approaches generate the strongest responses, so they can tailor future efforts from the knowledge gained. Metrics are an essential tool for librarians as the need for marketing increases. Often, librarians work within or without a confined budget and are asked to add "marketing guru" to an increasing list of professional skills.

A social marketing team of one is progressively taking precedent over advertising firms. As Viners develop a new kind of medium through instant videos that create a greater sense of interaction and presence, marketing firms are jumping on the phenomena produced from a single voice. Marketing trends are leaning toward an informal, responsive approach, and librarians can adapt analytics from their social media campaigns to maintain relevancy and introduce innovation to time-honored library promotion practices.

BRIEF HISTORY OF LIBRARY MARKETING IN THE TWENTY-FIRST CENTURY

Library marketing has conventionally held three tiers of campaign involvement: small, medium, and large. Small library marketing campaigns have included internal advertising of events and resources through signage, word-of-mouth promotion, book displays, and pamphlets. Medium marketing campaigns include outreach, the creation of library newsletters, and annual promotions such as Banned Books Week, Library Card Sign-Up Month, and Family History Month. Larger marketing campaigns encompass regular outreach and community representation and purchased advertising as well as scheduled promotions, internal signage, and leaflets.

While marketing has been viewed as a set of strategies and techniques that belong to partners or administrators outside of librarianship, the management process that identifies, anticipates, and supplies library users' requirements efficiently has organically occurred within the profession. Libraries have successfully developed a variety of creative and innovative promotion approaches ranging from positive public relations, interactive web presences, active advocacy, contests, Friends of the Library groups, public presentations and representation, blogs, podcasts, videos, and wikis (websites that allow collaborative editing of content and structure). Knowledgeable and enthusiastic library staff recognize their competence to work as promotional tools inside and outside of the physical library space as well as through the medium of mobile social marketing applications.

As librarians strive to keep up with breakthrough technology and remodel their marketing practices to include mobile outreach, library schools and the American Library Association work to provide resources and alter the perception of marketing in librarianship. The advent of mobile social marketing has added a domain of promotional outreach for librarians and solidified the onus for librarians to add marketing to their repertoire of professional skills. According to a recent Pew Report, *Library Services in the Digital Age*, one in five (22 percent) of Americans know "all or most" of what their public library offers, 46 percent know some of what's going on, and the remaining 31 percent are pretty much clueless.

Mobile social marketing applications are game changers as they increase the exposure of library promotion at relatively minimal cost. Resources, materials, and programming can be advertised through text, image, and video on high-traffic networks through popular devices, methods, and tags.

Increased exposure is the key to marketing success. Rarely are consumers sold on a product or service upon the initial introduction. Mobile social marketing applications offer increased exposure of library services on multiple platforms: Tumblr, Vine, Twitter, Instagram, Snapchat, and Facebook. Like persistent drops of water cutting into rock, mobile and fixed library marketing can be combined to offer optimum exposure.

LIBRARY MARKETING IS INHERENTLY MOBILE AND SOCIAL

Library marketing is inherently mobile and social because library services are fundamentally mobile and social. Circulation is by definition mobile. The concept of a shared collection of resources is a socialistic approach to share lifelong education, information access, and communal equity.

Taking library resources out into the community where users were active in society through the use of a bookmobile became a favored strategy in the United States in the 1800s. Traveling libraries became popular as horse-drawn carts, cars, and trucks were used to deliver books to community hubs or remote library locations. Mobile circulation of library materials were unencumbered with the technological limitations of integrated library systems. Vehicles could store books and materials as they traversed growing communities.

During the Great Depression the growth of public access libraries grew. In his article "The American Public Library during the Great Depression," author Charles Seavey opined what he called an American saying from the time of tumultuous economic downturn, "Libraries will get you through times with no money better than money will get you through times with no libraries." By 1925, the American Library Association established a Committee on Library Extension to bring library services to unserved or underserved areas throughout the country.

Libraries formed community outreach programs similar to government outreach programs to meet the needs of library users. Library programming turned its focus on social and equitable solutions to community needs. Services and library marketing were tailored to encourage use and meet the needs of particular groups within a local population such as job seekers and the African American community.

The Library Bill of Rights was produced in 1939 and cemented the social and mobility aspects of librarianship:

"I. Books and other library resources should be provided for the interest, information and enlightenment of all people of the community the library serves."

For the equitable benefit of society, the library collection should be assembled with the social and educational needs of all members in mind. Dialogue and exchange by means of published information is provided in a library composed of materials aggregated for every reader. Such a collection provides opportunities for individuals and groups to gather over information and sells the ideal of the library as community hub for the access and interchange of knowledge.

"II. Libraries should provide materials and information presenting all points of view on current and historical issues."

Social justice hinges on access to an unabridged record of human events. Engaging library users and potential library users requires a collection of materials and a knowledgeable staff, as well as facilities and policies that reflect the diversity of the library's service community.

Intellectual freedom, education, and democracy are among the highest ethics and values of the library profession. These principles are codified in the Library Bill of Rights and the Code of Ethics of the American Library Association. Libraries play a vital role in advancing the causes of social justice by offering uncensored worldviews to be studied, evolved, and eventually abandoned or applied.

"V. A person's right to use a library should not be denied or abridged because of origin, age, background or views."

Mobile library services are crucial in meeting the standards of the fifth article of the Library Bill of Rights. Access to information and resources cannot be countered because of socioeconomic status. Academic and philosophical divisions of the library field devote research to community informatics to determine where to build branches within a community to best serve all groups and meet needs of underprivileged members, how to advertise services to appeal and encourage use from various cultural and social backgrounds, and how to construct resources that are applicable and advantageous to the entire service community.

"VI. Libraries which make exhibit spaces and meeting rooms available to the public they serve should make such facilities (space, equipment, programming, and materials necessary to serve library users) available on an equitable basis, regardless of the beliefs or affiliations of individuals or groups requesting their use."

Making facilities available on an equitable basis suggests the inherent mobile and social qualities of librarianship. Ensuring that resources are modified to permit the largest range of access and use is an undertaking that proves challenging and rewarding when applied properly. The importance of mobile social marketing of library services is a conventional addition to the technological advances in library service that can help make facilities available on an increasingly equitable basis.

During World War II, nationalism and propaganda had strong ties to access of library resources and information. Posters and advertisements contrasted Third Reich book burnings against free library cards and services in the United States. The importance of public information and the sheer volume of knowledge held in a typical library came to light on the international stage. As Nazis assumed control over pockets of Europe, information was confiscated from public and private libraries. In fact, nearly one-third of books in German libraries were lost.

Newer nations established their eminence with national libraries and officiated collections to represent the library users of the twenty-first century. The independence of India and the success of the Tehran Conference contributed to the growth of libraries throughout the globe and invaluable contributions to librarianship from Eastern and Soviet institutions.

Collaboration is a core element of library service. The process of library mobility and socialization continues to change with society and technology. Connecting through reference transactions and shared learning is a primary goal for librarians and will continue to be integral to library use as patrons shape services to answer their needs.

2

GETTING STARTED WITH MOBILE SOCIAL MARKETING

Mobile social marketing is no longer a static practice that can be perfected quickly. As stated earlier, each day, four hundred million messages are shared through Snapchat alone. Instagram permits more than 130 million users to send photos and clips from their mobile devices. The six-second video-making app, Vine, has skyrocketed to forty million users within its first year and Tumblr has grown with mobile capabilities to reach more than 126.4 million users. App development is one of the largest-growing sectors of modern business. Marketing perception is rapidly transforming into a conversation between the library brand and its audience with over 20 percent of the global population owning a mobile device and available to connect with library services.

Before proceeding it is a great idea to develop a plan or strategy for how you will utilize these mobile social marketing applications in your library. What forms of marketing are you already leveraging and how can these tools help you achieve your overall goals? Let's talk about how to develop a mobile social marketing plan for your library.

DEVELOP A MOBILE SOCIAL MARKETING PLAN

The mobile social marketing plan for a library will be similar to its web or mobile site design plan. A library's mobile presence should be as intrinsically united with the physical library space as the library's online domain. Major themes will be purported in all three venues of the physical space, the library website, and the library's mobile social networks.

For example, the library's service objectives should be clear. Academic and special libraries devote more space in their structures to their collections. If the library devotes significant resources and time to showcasing its holdings, then a mobile social marketing objective should be to share the library's collection on its network accounts. An ideal use of mobile social networks in relation to library marketing is to complement current practices and to take information further via mobile means.

Invite ideas from all members of staff engaged in promotion. If a youth services librarian has been tasked with creating press releases for annual story times and children's events, ascertain what language and methods of entreaty have been useful in the past. Mobile social marketing lends itself to enhancing current library marketing and tailoring the library's message to meet mobile readers.

The scope of a mobile social marketing plan will detail the objective, intended reach, level of interaction, regularity of use, and staffing of each mobile social network. Each mobile social network may be unique in these details as it is determined how to best serve a library service community. Consider the community and the skill set and resources available on staff, and make sure the short- and long-term marketing targets are taken into account when drafting a mobile social marketing plan.

For example, the objective on a library's Twitter account may be to reach community groups already active on Twitter. The community's radio stations, newspapers, and civic organizations are excellent audience groups to advertise to and may be worthy of the investment of a library Twitter account. The objective of a library's Instagram account may be to reach a younger, more mobile audience or to share stories when pictures are significantly stronger than words. If a library receives an anonymous donation in the book return, Instagram offers a real-time, intimate quality to share this news as opposed to Facebook. The library's objective needs to be clear as it will influence all other aspects of a library's mobile social marketing plan.

Audience and Reach

The intended reach of a library's mobile social network is crucial to tracking its success. Determining the intended reach of a mobile social platform requires some research. How many users in a specific age range use this particular mobile social network? How many users living in the community's service area are registered users of this particular mobile social network? What time of day do other companies and organizations post on this particular mobile social network? When is the observed height of use of this particular mobile social network during an average business day? All these factors will guide a library's use and intended reach.

For example, the average age of Tumblr users is 34.6 years old. Programs on family planning, buying a home, and job seeking will appeal to a library's Tumblr audience more than posts concerning senior events and early literacy services. Recent metrics suggest Tumblr users are more active during Sunday than any other day of the week. Nearly half of all Tumblr activity occurs between 5:00 p.m. and 1:00 a.m. throughout the week. Posting to Tumblr on Sunday, even if the library is closed, in the late evening may be a library's best bet on reaching its audience.

Level of Interaction

Level of interaction is crucial in mobile social marketing planning. Much of the magic in mobile social marketing is the ability to have one-on-one conversations with a marketing audience. Allowing the marketing audience to post to the library's space is a scary concept for many library professionals. Public services invite innumerable views. These views have to potential to show support for a library's services or challenge the carefully constructed marketing narrative of the library. Soliciting interaction on social media will amplify the public's perception on the library. Referring to the library's policy on posting signage and solicitation is a good start to setting parameters on a mobile social network. Libraries may wish to refer to legal counsel to ascertain what constitutes a post that is legal to remove from the library's mobile social network if needs be.

Staffing

Library staff should be briefed on copyright as well as the library's official marketing narrative to ensure that posts are consistently free from abuse and represent the library's mobile social marketing plan. Frequency of checking the network for user comments can be set in the plan and made easier through the use of the network's notification options. Determining which staff member or members will "like" comments, respond to questions, and ultimately follow up with communication through private messaging or even the deletion of a post should be explained in the mobile social marketing plan.

Staffing the library's mobile social marketing plan is crucial to setting standards, creating marketing campaigns, and tracking success. Librarians should be encouraged to follow their library's mobile social networks and engage with users through mobile social networks if they have an acumen for conversing with mobile apps. It is common for librarians to be stopped at their local grocery, church, or gym by service community members to be asked about programs or to offer impromptu device instruction. Mobile social networks have only increased access to library staff in this unofficial way. A strong mobile social marketing plan can help librarians navigate off-the-clock reference and quantify this type of outreach and marketing to be useful in library marketing, annual reports, and strategic planning.

Workflow and Regularity of Use

Regularity of use is another aspect of a library's mobile social marketing plan. Beyond personal interaction with a marketing audience, mobile social marketing permits libraries to post real-time events. The beauty of sharing information on mobile social networks such as Instagram, Snapchat, Vine, or Tumblr is how it transforms communication into an immediate, intimate experience. Librarians can opt to post to networks a few times a week and even schedule posts to go out at certain times of the day; however, wiggle room for authentic sharing should be incorporated into a library's mobile social marketing plan.

For example, a political figure may drop by a library facility, which could be shared with the community service through Snapchat. Mobile social network posts advertise that the library is a living, breathing community space with many happenings. Sometimes these happenings can be shared and advertised in advance. Other times they can only be imparted on the fly. Another great example of real-time mobile social marketing is posts of participants at library events. When an Instagram picture of crafternoons for first graders or a Vine of seniors singing with a local musician are posted during the program, it speaks of the library's vibrancy and asks the audience, "Do you see what you are missing?"

Planning Committee

An ideal committee for mobile social marketing planning would be two or three members of staff. Mobile social groups with more than three members tend to veer off track and lose focus of the major elements of a library mobile social marketing plan: objectives, intended reach, level of interaction, regularity of use, and staffing. However, with step-by-step instructions, adherence to successful marketing practices already in play, and a well-defined plan, an effective mobile social marketing team of one is obtainable.

3

TOOLS AND APPLICATIONS

What are mobile social marketing apps? Mobile social marketing applications generally refer to two different things: a mobile website and a native app. A mobile website is a mobile phone-friendly site created with cellular access in mind. Typically, a mobile website will have a layout best viewed from a small screen, have visual signposts, and be populated with content that can be downloaded quickly. A native app is a specifically manufactured platform that can be downloaded through mobile app stores. For the purposes of this instruction, mobile social marketing apps refer to the native apps built by companies, such as Tumblr, or mobile social entities that exist solely as native apps, such as Snapchat.

Each application to be examined has distinct features that support library marketing purposes. Snapchat, Instagram, Vine, and Tumblr are like other library services and can serve librarians and their users concurrently or individually.

The privacy level of each application varies and alters when blended with other mobile apps. Mobile social applications are microcultures built on a foundation of axiomatic, social network conventions but each has distinct user behaviors and expectations. Best practices incorporate a thorough examination of the privacy policy of mobile social marketing applications. To ensure cohesive marketing, the level of privacy should be determined before posting.

SNAPCHAT

Snapchat is a photo messaging application. Users of Snapchat can take photos and record videos, add text and drawings to the footage captured, and send them to a controlled list of recipients. Photographs and videos sent are known as "snaps." Users set a time limit for how long recipients can view their snaps, from one to ten seconds. After the snaps have been viewed for the permitted time, they are concealed from the recipients' devices and deleted from Snapchat's servers. Snapchat has the advantage of personal access to private lives for a new, more intimate marketing experience.

Whether it is a best-selling title or one-on-one database instruction, library services are commonly sought out by users in a time of immediate want or need and then forgotten. Applications like Snapchat can introduce library services to users in an instant fashion that plants a seed of want or awareness. Onetime library events or ongoing library services can be strategically shared on Snapchat at the peak of their use and popularity.

Third-Party Apps

Several third-party applications will store Snapchat snaps with and without the consent or knowledge of the sender. Apple hosts third-party complimentary applications for Snapchat such as SnapRoll and SnapBox. SnapRoll allows users to save their snaps, photos, and video to their camera roll. SnapRoll also permits camera roll photos and video, which can also be altered by photo and filter apps, to be used for snaps.

SnapBox is a third-party Snapchat container app that permits users to save each snap they receive. This application does not inform the senders of snaps when their receivers have chosen to save the content shared through Snapchat.

Android's SnapChat Save Pic operates much like a Snapchat overlay with a similar layout and menu choices. SnapChat Save Pic essentially replaces the official Snapchat app on a user's device. The one remarkable feature is the download option to save Snaps sent to the user's device. SnapChat Save Pic also acts as a container application which will automatically save each Snap the user creates and sends.

ProSnap is a third-party application used for Windows devices, laptops, and computers. As long as the hardware has a camera, users can see and send snaps through their Snapchat account via ProSnap.

INSTAGRAM

In the world of mobile social marketing, an Instagram picture is worth significantly more than a thousand words. The right photograph or clip can amount to thousands of comments, shares, and likes. A marketing audience responds to visual storytelling through infographics, GIFs (graphic interchange format supporting both animated and static images), and pictures today as much as in the golden age of *Mad Men* with meticulous, hand-painted advertisements.

Humanize library promotion using Instagram, the mobile photo- and video-sharing social network. Provide instant accounts of library programming, new books, and resources to the ever-growing membership of the social media powerhouse, Instagram. Gather and share visual depictions of service and accomplishment with the public rather than just a board of trustees or a supervisor.

Libraries the world over are utilizing Instagram to share their stories. The City of London's Barbican Library posts their flyers of upcoming events, pictures of browsers at their summer pop-up library set up outdoors, and images of ongoing displays. A tremendous sense of the community as well as the Barbican Library's role therein is imparted to their Instagram followers, at home and abroad.

Instagram makes engagement through brief, imaginative posts possible. Create an Instagram to market to an audience of current and potential users and keep the organization brand in the relevant realms of dialogue.

Third-Party Apps

Third-party applications for Instagram allow users to view Instagram pics on the web (web.stagram.com), view and tag pics by geographical location (Instamap), and gather statistical data on their account and posts (Statigram).

Instagram web viewers like Webstagram allow users to navigate the mobile platform from a computer. Instagram members can sign into their account, view the photos on the accounts they follow, comment and like photos, browse tags, and follow/unfollow other Instagram accounts. Webstagram can be used as an instructional resource to teach non-mobile users about mobile social networks and allows broader access to the library's social network administrators.

Ink361 is another Instagram web viewer that allows account holders to view photos online, create infographic handouts of Instagram likes, gather analytics, create notifications to be alerted to likes and followers, and organize images with tags and folders.

Filter and frame apps give users more options before they post to Instagram. iOS third-party apps to enhance photographs include InstaCollage, which has 2-D and 3-D clip art and caption additions, and InstaFrame to merge photos of various sizes and shapes into one cohesive image. Embellishments to Instagram pics can help libraries accomplish a professional tone on their account and can amplify the storytelling element for each picture shared with library stakeholders.

Instamap supports same-time browsing of Instagram uploads by geographical location and through the tags used to describe the image. Instamap allows librarians to narrow down what images are trending in their community, practically down to the borough or neighborhood.

Statigram gives Instagram users their total number of likes received, an account of most liked photos during the lifetime of the account, and the average number of likes and comments per photo as well as follower growth charts and analytics.

Android's approach to third-party apps for Instagram is to explore the boundaries of the social medium. Applications like Textgram create images from text to share on Instagram. Clip art, filters, and inspirational quotes inspire users to revert to text when using the imaged-based network. Textgram is useful for book quotes or library quotes that can be shared with library followers and can connect Instagram posts automatically to a library's Facebook and Flickr (a photo social network) accounts.

Instagram Follower Tracker is an application that allows libraries to monitor the reach of their Instagram account. This tracker shows daily tallies of lost and gained followers and allows a user to follow or unfollow other Instagram accounts accordingly.

DO IT FOR THE VINE

Ready. Set. Action! Breaking through the limited attention span of today's digital audience can be a challenge. However, Vine, a video-based social network owned by Twitter, grabs the attentions of users accustomed to 140 characters or less to sell an idea. Vine is a fun alternative to traditional marketing that allows users to share and exchange minivideos in a rapid, same-time pace.

Vine is a video-sharing service and social network application. Vine allows users to record and edit six-second-long looping video clips called "vines." Users of Vine, who are called Viners, can search for other users and content, comment on Vines, and revine other users' posts to share with their followers.

The average attention span of a person is seven seconds. Six-second vines are more social, shareable, and direct alternatives to typical instruction videos found on a library's website or YouTube page. Libraries can transform the basic introduction of tools and resources by creatively filming information in short intervals.

Follow the commercial success of companies like Starburst and Adidas through the mobile social network Vine. Gain new followers, provide insight into programming and services in new, exciting venues, and keep current on the methodology of informational exchange.

Vine offers engagement through short, innovative posts that can be commented upon, shared with other accounts, and viewed repeatedly. By creating a Vine account to market to an audience, appeal to current and potential users is added and the brand of the organization is kept fresh.

Third-Party Apps

Many web-based Vine viewers are available for users and nonusers to watch vines from devices without mobile capabilities. VineViewer.co allows visitors to view vines that are popular and trending as well as search vines by usernames and tags. Canopy is another Vine browser for Microsoft Surface, Google, and Android users with limited searching options.

Apple has authorized numerous third-party applications to augment Vines. Vinyet has one of the broadest ranges of options as it includes the potential to upload video from the user's camera roll; edit, splice, and compress video; lay filters on the video; and add music to the video before directly uploading it to Vine.

VineGrab is a Vine container application that allows users to save their vines and other users' vines to their camera roll. Vine container applications like VineGrab can allow Viners to save Vine queries or comments from library followers to refer to in order to reply at a later time. VineGrab manages multiple accounts for librarians operating a personal and professional profile on Vine.

TUMBLR

Tumblr is a microblogging platform and social networking website that has been increasingly adopted as a social marketing application. Tumblr enables users to post multimedia and other content to a short-form blog. Users can follow blogs, search for content, reblog, comment on blogs, and "like" blogs ("heart" blogs similar to a Facebook thumbs-up).

Telling the library's services narrative through articles, images, GIFs, and walls of text can be competently accomplished with a Tumblr account. Libraries on Tumblr can break down services and engage individual demographics such as teens, book clubs, or study groups. Tumblr's platform, which authorizes the use of multimedia, generates highly shareable content as vivid posts are captured, altered, and shared.

TWITTER

Twitter is a social network that permits users to communicate through brief 140-character messages that may also include GIFs, images, and videos. Twitter is unique in its access for registered and unregistered users. Users of Twitter with registered accounts can post, follow other users, favorite (like) tweets, and retweet. Nonregistered users on Twitter can search for accounts and terms and view Twitter accounts with open privacy settings.

Libraries are using Twitter to establish a connection with users and claim their space in the service community's digital sphere. Librarians on Twitter comment on upcoming programming; respond to news in the publishing, film, and music industries; create opportunities for professional development; and reinforce immediate and responsive marketing strategies to engage and inform.

Mobile social marketing plans should include Twitter for its strengths in rapid search and response to information as well as its multimedia sharing power. Librarians can boost library news by hopping onto an appropriately trending tag, by sharing images and videos of services, and by keeping users in the know with live tweeting sessions during library events.

Third-Party Apps

Hootsuite is a social media manager that serves the users of Twitter well. Hootsuite permits Twitter users to manage multiple accounts including Facebook, LinkedIn, Google+, Foursquare, Myspace, and WordPress. With its dashboard interface, mobile social moderators and content producers can review several networks at once while making updates. Hootsuite offers much of its product line for free and has won several Open Web Awards as it continues to develop and make available social administration technology.

Talon for Twitter is a third-party Twitter client. Beyond tweeting, searching, and tagging, which can be done with the stock Twitter application, Talon has integration features for other social networks and supports the operation of separate accounts. Librarians can toggle between their library's Twitter and their own account with one swipe. Talon Pull is a feature that permits users to access their Twitter feed without opening the app. Talon Pull is essentially a live feed of tweets that appears in the device's notifications center and allows users to check Twitter with a single tap.

Janetter is a third-party Twitter client that has applications for iPhone and Android devices. Unique features from Janetter include an unread tweet manager to help users catch up on the tweets of the day, pop-up translation for tweets written in different languages, a multiple-line viewer of Twitter walls to review tweet conversations, and real-time tweet updates.

Janetter is a helpful application for event tweeting during library programming or at library conferences for users to keep up with the information being shared. This client can be applied during #libchat discussions scheduled by librarians around the world to assist in tracking library-related tags and translating the thoughts of libraries in languages all around the globe.

FACEBOOK

Facebook is currently the most popular mobile social networking application and boasts more than 890 million active daily users. Facebook's services permit users to connect with other Facebook accounts by finding and adding them as friends. Users can post text, images, and videos; create groups and events for activities; and upload photo and video albums as well as like and comment on the posts of others.

Libraries are using Facebook as a primary access point for information on library events, programming, collections, and services. Librarians provide reader's advisory, directional and instructional guidance, and ready reference through their official Facebook pages. Librarians can utilize Facebook functions to create book club groups, share new materials as they come available for users, and link directly on Facebook to drive users to the library's website and digital collections.

Third-Party Apps

Flipster is an interface-focused client that makes Facebook content minimalistic and easier to browse. Like most Facebook clients working against Facebook's limitation on third-party apps, Flipster is limited to the customization of existing functional content. Flipster allows Facebook users to edit their menus and adjust content to meet personal operational needs as users alter font, text size, and color of Facebook feed.

Paper is a standalone mobile application created by Facebook. Paper transforms Facebook content into a format that resembles a hard-copy media such as a newspaper, book, or magazine. The burgeoning use of Facebook lends to the innovation of content customization for a visually aesthetic search. Facebook users need assistance in reading and assessing so much information.

Browsing through Facebook content is made easier with Paper as it dissects status updates to chapters or sections. Users can divide status updates into sections such as sports, politics, and entertainment for effortless perusal. Users can create their own segments for items concerning local news, family, and personal interest, too.

Facebook Groups is another application developed by Facebook. Facebook Groups allows users to view all their Facebook groups in one place without the distraction of a Facebook wall, pages, and messages. Users can create and find new groups, chat within groups, and post content to groups. If a library anticipates adding the use of Facebook Groups into its mobile social marketing plan, adding this app on the library's mobile devices should be considered. Facebook Groups is a tool that can help librarians accomplish their mobile social promotion and content management tasks.

4

LIBRARY EXAMPLES AND CASE STUDIES

CHATTANOOGA PUBLIC LIBRARY'S VINE

In 2013, the Chattanooga Public Library created an official Vine account. In part, the library's expanding social media presence was designed to meet the digital and communication objectives of the Chattanooga Public Library's strategic plan. The purpose of the Chattanooga Public Library Vine began as public exploration of new media (short-video sharing was a relatively new concept for social media marketing at the time) and the engagement of other Vine users within the library's community.

The Chattanooga Public Library in Chattanooga, Tennessee, serves Hamilton County, which is composed of more than 336,463 residents. The library has grown notoriety for its digital content collection, renovation on the physical library space, and service models to remain relevant to modern library users. Their Vine account (https://vine.co/venues/4d6e839a3836370497cfa9d0) depicts the library's excellence in programming and features many service points of the library's second floor, including an arcade, recording studio, and makerspace with 3-D printer access.

Purpose

The Chattanooga Public Library's strategic plan was a collaboration of library staff, the Library Board, and Friends of the Chattanooga Public

Library as well as stakeholders throughout the community. The strategic planning sessions discovered a need for dynamic and sustainable outreach through mobile social marketing networks and emphasized access to current technology. The intention of all social media networks representing the Chattanooga Public Library is to solicit support for library services while making the community aware of what the library has to offer them.

Scope

The Chattanooga Public Library's Vine organically shifted marketing to teens and others featuring the services provided on the second floor of the library's physical space. Organically, other libraries, makerspaces, and maker groups have followed the Chattanooga Public Library's Vines, which predominately showcase makers using library resources to create. Most of the Vine posts show various projects completed at library programs such as crafts, music, and robotics. Occasionally Vines are tagged with popular maker hashtags such as #NationofMakers and #CitizenScience.

Justin Hoenke, who is also known by his online persona, Justin the Librarian, is the coordinator of teen services as well as manager of the second floor of the Chattanooga Public Library. His background in librarianship, digital content creation, and STEAM (science, technology, engineering, arts, and math) programming make him a well-rounded contributor to the library's Vine. Each ten-second clip narrates an exciting and diverse range of library events. The library Vine is closely tied together with Hoenke's account as he drives followers from his profile to the library's by reposting his experiences onto the Chattanooga Public Library's wall.

Best Practices

The Vines that record aspects of the Chattanooga's Public Library's makerspace are the most popular. Makerspace Vines experience more reposts and likes than any other content. As the library staff discovered a pattern of interest, they continued to share the user experience on the second floor, and in particular at the makerspace.

Reviewing the appeal of mobile social marketing posts is essential. Learning what an audience responds to and then centering their marketing content for the broadest reach has been a practice of the Chattanooga Library staff. Cross posting on multiple social media platforms or setting networks to sync posts has been a helpful tool to form long-term campaigns.

The Chattanooga Public Library has strong policies on Internet use and safety. Posts to their Vine account as well as other networks like Facebook, Instagram, and Twitter are inclusive as they follow the library's mission to enhance the ability to inspire, create, and dream.

Resources

The Chattanooga Public Library staff collaborate with many community initiatives that influence their approach to digital learning and mobile social marketing. Mozilla's Hive Learning Networks have established nontraditional learning environments for Chattanooga Library users and have fresh tactics for finding audiences through mobile networks. Immediate updates on their work can be discovered through the hashtag #HiveBuzz when searching on Vine, Instagram, Twitter, Tumblr, and Facebook.

Beyond the Chattanooga Library's Vine, other libraries utilizing Vine include the District of Columbia Public Library, the Chicago Public Library's YouMedia Center Vine, the Seattle Public Library Vine, and the Los Angeles Public Library Vine.

OSKALOOSA PUBLIC LIBRARY'S TEEN ZONE TUMBLR

The Oskaloosa Public Library in Oskaloosa, Iowa, serves nearly eleven thousand residents. Services for babies, preschoolers, tweens, teens, adults, and seniors are available through collections, programming, and events. Oskaloosa is the only public library in Mahaska County (population 22,335) located one hour from Iowa's state capital, Des Moines. In 2012, the library created a Teen Zone Tumblr (http://oskaloosalibrary.tumblr.com/) to use for teen program marketing.

Purpose

For the Oskaloosa Public Library, the motivation to join and use Tumblr was threefold:

1. To extend the library's reach through social media
2. To network with a teen audience in their natural online environment
3. To dedicate a platform to teens and post about teen services and programs

The director of the Oskaloosa Public Library, William Ottens, observed that many teens were not using Facebook, and those that were, did not interact with Facebook pages. To provide a place for mobile interaction that appealed to teen library patrons, Ottens surveyed the Oskaloosa Public Library's Teen Advisory Board and learned that some of the teens were on Tumblr.

Director Ottens is no stranger to the inner workings of Tumblr. His own Tumblr account, Librarian Problems (http://librarianproblems.com) has had much acclaim throughout the library profession. His Tumblr design of pop-culture-reference GIFs to describe the elations and frustrations of everyday librarianship is deeply relatable and is reverberated online as reposts to Tumblr, a Facebook page with more than 11,000 likes, and a Twitter account.

However, the Teen Zone Tumblr, named after the Teen Zone within the Oskaloosa Public Library, was not a commercial success until a creative work-study student from the area high school volunteered to take on the task of mobile social marketing. The student was an aspiring photographer and came up with many different ways to promote the library through photos she posted. The library was pleased to use local resources to build a direct and genuine Tumblr for teens.

Scope

While the primary scope of the Teen Zone Tumblr is to communicate with teens served by the Oskaloosa Public Library, their followers are now primarily other libraries and bookish accounts. Most of the Tumblr posts are of general book-related content or reblogs. The Tumblr is promoted through the Oskaloosa Public Library's Facebook and Twitter accounts on occasion. Actual Oskaloosa teens make up a small percentage of the Teen Zone Tumblr's following, as the library tried to engage them without hitting them over the head with marketing attempts.

The importance of maintaining a space to represent the teen demographic is essential. The Oskaloosa Public Library is an active mobile social presence that suggests its commitment to teen librarianship to the most unassuming visitor to their Tumblr. Oskaloosa Public Library's presence on Tumblr has helped them to connect with teens as well as professionals, create a learning opportunity for talented students, and continue to be an avenue to market the library.

Social Marketing Policy

The library director collaborated with the Library Board to develop a social media policy. The Oskaloosa Public Library's social marketing policy is viewed by staff as a legal reference in the case of deleting comments or blocking an individual from library social media accounts. Social media guidelines and policy differ among public libraries and academic libraries and within districts.

The director and youth librarian are the chief contributors to the Oskaloosa Public Library social media accounts. Rather than using a social media calendar, mobile social marketing is part of each planning, programming, and events conversation. Rather than establishing a long-range social marketing plan, the staff have worked to develop a unique voice to which their community responds well. Their voice is fresh, fluid, and conversational.

Best Practices

The Oskaloosa Public Library social media team considers a post to be really successful if it can engage followers and market library services. In their experience, posts that are clear announcements of what's happening at the library typically do not gain a lot of attention.

Quotes about books or reading actually receive a lot of likes and reblogs. Their work-study student took photographs of books, displays, the building, and the library reading garden, which gained a good number of likes and reblogs. In response to the positive reception to the posts, the library created a "Fun Fact about Your Library" series of updates that feature historical or lesser-known facts about the building or library services.

The Oskaloosa Public Library cross promotes all mobile social content throughout its networks. Marketing content that originates on their Tumblr is shared on their Facebook and Twitter as well. The staff have observed great response from cross promotion and credit their Tumblr's reach as well as boosting/reposting other library accounts.

Advice

Staff at the Oskaloosa Public Library advise to follow and interact with other libraries. Learn from what other libraries are doing. Reblog and like their posts and have fun with social media. A natural and engaging social marketing interaction hinges on staff buy-in. If staff are enjoying themselves, it will come through to their mobile social marketing audience.

When embarking on a social media marketing campaign, glean information from the demographic audience. Find a teen volunteer, work-study student, or Teen Advisory Board member to give great ideas on how to connect to teens in the library service community. Find a senior to liaise between the library and pages, groups, and mobile social hangouts for area seniors.

Resources

Oskaloosa staff closely follow the work of Kate Tkacik (thelifeguardlibrarian.tumblr.com), Matt Anderson (mattanderson.org), Karen Jenson (teenlibrariantoolbox.com), and Susan Brown (658point8.com). These social marketing gurus of the library world are prolific and generous with their ideas.

Library Journal and *School Library Journal*'s the Digital Shift are also valuable resources for the social media team. Beyond the library's regular subscriptions and RSS feeds, the director at Oskaloosa likes to check in on comparable and larger libraries for inspiration. Some of the libraries that the Oskaloosa Public Library models its mobile social marketing after include the Lawrence Public Library (Lawrence, Kansas), Darien Library (Darien, Connecticut), Arlington Public Library

(Arlington, Virginia), Davenport Public Library (Davenport, Iowa), and the New York Public Library.

GUILDHALL LIBRARY TWITTER

The Guildhall Library is a public reference library within the heart of London. It provides millions of users with access to digital collections as well as to a massive archive spanning centuries of local history. The Guildhall Library was founded in the 1420s and holds the largest collection devoted to the history of a single city in the world. Guildhall Library's main services are access to local business information (the library shares a building with the City of London's Business Library), regular lectures and workshops, City of London walking tours, and ongoing exhibitions. Under the authority of the City of London Corporation, the Guildhall Library is one of seven libraries of the historical Square Mile within the heart of central London.

Purpose

The goals of the Guildhall Library's Twitter account are manifold:

- Connect with users through mobile social media
- Promote special collections, services, and events
- Share news and timely announcements related to the Square Mile
- Distinguish the Guildhall Library from the other six City of London libraries

Each library under the remit of the City of London Corporation brings unique collections, services, and opportunities to their users. The Guildhall Library's Twitter (https://twitter.com/GuildhallLib) permits library staff to focus mobile marketing for their individual events while granting the occasion to cross promote interlibrary collaborations.

Scope

The intended reach of the Guildhall Library's Twitter is current and potential users of Guildhall Library services. Videos, images, and text sharing the library's holdings, going behind the scenes with library staff, and promotion of upcoming events are the typical topics of marketing content.

Social Marketing Policy

The Guildhall Library's social marketing policy may be one of the most comprehensive as it shares the policy with all of the City of London Corporation, which comprises the mayor of London's office and the municipal governing body of London. The main social media networks used by the City of London are Twitter, Facebook, YouTube, LinkedIn, and audioBoom.

Their social media strategy includes training appropriate staff (social media moderators) on relevant and new social media networks and standardization of the conduct and criteria of posts. Social media updates are geared to market learning opportunities, inform users of services, and encourage communication.

Best Practices

The Guildhall Library's tweets that feature images of the library's collection and exhibition have the furthest reach. Followers of the library retweet, favorite, and respond to picture tweets more than any other content.

Long-term campaigns such as the 450th anniversary of William Shakespeare's birthday (or the 398th anniversary of his death) are a source of interest to the library's Twitter followers. Programs throughout the City were promoted on the library's accounts as well as the library's series of events: walks and talks, visits to memorials of Shakespeare's life on the north bank of London, and performances of some of his sonnets. Rubber ducks depicting the Bard were made available for purchase during the monthlong campaign and featured in several tweets as the Shakespeare duck enjoyed various Guildhall Library services.

Advice

The staff at the Guildhall Library (working as social media moderators) suggest friendly and natural communication for the mobile social library market. Even when handling something as sacred as a copy of Shakespeare's first folio, humanizing the interaction with a rubber ducky and ensuring the information makes a relevant connection to the audience is crucial. When informing social media followers of library services, make the information relate to them in today's terms.

THE MORGAN LIBRARY AND MUSEUM INSTAGRAM

The Morgan Library and Museum in New York City began as the private library of financier Pierpont Morgan. The collection consists of early editions of printed books and old master drawings and paintings as well as literary and historical manuscripts. In 1924, Pierpont's son J. P. Morgan made the library of cultural treasures available to scholars and the public as a public institution.

The mission of the Morgan Library and Museum is "to preserve, build, study, present, and interpret a collection of extraordinary quality, in order to stimulate enjoyment, excite the imagination, advance learning, and nurture creativity." In 2014, the Morgan Library created an official Instagram account (https://instagram.com/themorganlibrary/) to share the beautiful visages that are typical to the daily routine of preservation at the Morgan Library and Museum.

Purpose

The purpose of the Morgan Library and Museum's Instagram account is to support the institution's mission in presenting a collection for enjoyment and study. Posts include pieces from the collection, visitor activities, and promotions for upcoming events.

Scope

All demographics of the Morgan Library and Museum users, the entire collection, and every service is promoted through their Instagram account. Information regarding the Morgan Campus, visiting hours, amenities, and scheduling a tour of special collections is handled through the Morgan Library's social networks equally. Instagram posts are synced to display on the Morgan's Facebook and Twitter accounts to share the information provided through images as available to mobile social media users.

Best Practices

Instagram updates that tell a story of staff or participant interaction with each other and the collection are incredibly popular with the Morgan Library and Museum's followers. During the holidays, Morgan staffers make creative cards illustrating pieces of the collection and ask followers to share their own creations with the hashtag #MorganHandmade.

Similarly, the Morgan Library and Museum gains much mobile social marketing attention by reposting the digital word of mouth of other Instagram users' photos of the library, the museum, and its events. When visitors post images of the magnificent architecture, the staff reposts and tags the Morgan Library. In turn, the original poster typically replies, as do other witnesses and institutional users who share content.

Previews or sneak peeks of upcoming exhibitions offer behind-the-scenes looks at the collection and library services as well as whet the appetite of users. Linking preview images to the Morgan Library and Museum's website or event registration page drives users from their Instagram account to more information available online. Building excitement and then giving users somewhere to go with that momentum is a best practice supplied by the staff at the Morgan.

MASHABLE'S SNAPCHAT

Mashable is a news website offering the latest information on digital innovation, online trends, and mobile devices. In the early days of Snapchat's launch, Mashable developed a team of staff to explore and experiment with the mobile social platform. The official Mashable Snapchat (username: mashable) uses a happenstance approach to marketing. Using popular cultural references, Mashable shares one- to ten-second stories about National Cheese Day, the 2012 presidential election, the 150th anniversary of Central Park's opening, and even the Discovery Channel's Shark Week.

Purpose

While libraries are figuring out how to use Snapchat for library promotion, Mashable has visualized clear purposes for its Snapchat account, purposes that can be adopted and adapted for mobile social library marketing:

- Learning the ins and outs of mobile social trends
- Experimenting with the boundaries and possibilities of emerging technology
- Staking claim of its brand in this specific mobile social arena
- Developing strategies to use and share with customers and Snapchat followers

Although most tech news outlets like Mashable predicted the success of Snapchat, the company had little to lose in the investment of time and research. Reviewing the methods and avenues of mobile communication is a strategy for strong, meaningful marketing.

Scope

As a major tech news source, Mashable has a considerable scope. Its current and future subscribers, professionals in advertising, social media and digital progression, and mobile social marketing librarians, are within the scope of Mashable's Snapchat.

Mashable's scope directs its content differently than the scope of a library account. Users following Mashable snaps hope to glean information about the process of productively sharing on Snapchat. A library's Snapchat audience seeks information on resources useful to them on a consumer level such as programs, new materials, and events.

Social Marketing Strategy

Mashable's social marketing strategy is founded on driving visitors to their news site. As a guide to digital culture, Mashable harnesses mobile social media networks to encourage users to seek information from its banner as it engages through current topics on tech user interest. Mashable's social media marketing base includes an audience of over three million on Facebook, more than five million followers on Twitter, and nearly 1.5 million followers on Pinterest.

Best Practices

Teachable moments create a powerful marketing influence. Unlike Instagram posts, Vines, or tweets, snaps are brief moments of flashing information. Rather than seeking feedback, snaps give data in creative, witty, or humorous ways.

For the 150th anniversary of Central Park's opening, Mashable snapped photos of scenes from famous movies that took place in Central Park. The momentary nods to creative layering of visual information and to the filmographic history and the cultural implications of Central Park don't ask users directly for much more than a like or a share. Adept users discover ways to save the posts and boost Mashable on more permanent social media platforms.

Advice

Staff who post for Mashable advise authenticity through public and private social media accounts. Whether sharing glimpses inside the day-to-day workings at the Mashable offices or behind-the-stanchions coverage of major tech releases, Mashable snaps denote genuine interest in the work of sharing tech news.

Enthusiasm is easily detectable in mobile social marketing and often difficult to fabricate. Authentic voices and approaches toward teachable moments will help Snapchat users to engage and retain an audience through relatable promotion of relevant information. Long-range mobile social marketing may seem like a one-sided conversation at the start but can develop into dialogue and useful interchange through a sharing, liking, and reposting ripple effect.

5

STEP-BY-STEP LIBRARY PROJECTS FOR MOBILE SOCIAL MARKETING

- How to Create Tumblr Pages for the Library
- How to Use Snapchat for Library Social Media Marketing
- How to Provide Reader's Advisory through Instagram
- How to Use Instagram for Library Marketing
- How to Use Vine for Library Instruction
- How to Host a Library Contest for Twitter
- How to Create a Facebook Group for a Library Book Club

This collection of interactive mobile social marketing projects for the mobile social platforms Snapchat, Vine, Instagram, and Tumblr as well as successful examples from others in the profession can be used as a guide to develop a new marketing campaign, provide insight to staff and stakeholders, and supply inspiration and stratagems to tweak existing marketing practices. Because exchange through mobile social networks is a common practice for the greater portion of library users, each example and case study is applicable to libraries great and small, rural and urban, public and private.

HOW TO CREATE TUMBLR PAGES FOR THE LIBRARY

Tumblr is a combination of a social network and a microblogging platform. Although Tumblr has been around since 2007, it began to hit its stride with the onset of mobile applications. By May 2013, Tumblr boasted more than 188.7 million blogs and was purchased by Yahoo! Inc. for $1.1 billion.

The Tumblr interface has improved with mobile modification. Tumblr's dashboard gives users access to post content, share or reblog other users' posts, like or "heart" other users' posts, and manage account settings. Much like Facebook's wall, Tumblr users scroll through multimedia content such as text, photos, quotes, links, chats, and video in the structure of short-form blogs.

Follow the path but set the trend by microblogging through Tumblr. Librarians are finding their teens and new adults on the multimedia, mobile social network as they share attractive posts on books, music, television, films, art, politics, and popular culture. Tumblr, stylized as tumblr., is a steadily growing social network for libraries, companies, organizations, sports teams, governments, members of royalty, celebrities, and more.

Learn the power of the GIF to appeal to digital citizens brought up in the Internet age who employ sound and sight to convey dozens of mobile messages each day. While Tumblr is not the typical blogging structure used by pundits or globetrotter diarists, it takes the principle of informational discussion online and condenses thought into manageable, rebloggable concepts.

How to Create a Teen Library Tumblr

Technology trends studies show teens moving in droves away from Twitter and Facebook to be replaced with mobile networks like Instagram and Tumblr. While Tumblr is highly popular, it is not in the mainstream use of teachers, grandparents, and parents. Teens are drawn to mobile social platforms that seem newer and exclusive. Teen librarians can tap into this subculture of mobile library users through a responsive Tumblr account.

Several major libraries and library associations use Tumblr to connect with colleagues and spread information about the library science field. Other libraries share Teen Advisory Board, Teen Anime Club, the library Sit and Stitch Group, and the Friends of the Library information as individual blogs devoted to the respective group's activities. Tapping into Tumblr's quirks, memes, and running jokes can help librarians continue to connect with teens and can help teens relate to library news when it is marketing in a fashion that speaks to their experience.

Adding a Tumblr account into a library's marketing strategy issues more than a seasonal dalliance with the social network de jour but rather a deep exploration into the nuances of current social media exchange. The knowledge gained from a library Tumblr account can issue important reference exchanges on social media use, online privacy, and digital communication and provide a valuable space for Tumblr users in the library's service community.

Getting Started

Determine how Tumblr fits into a library's marketing policies and procedures before creating an account. Will the library as a whole be represented or would Tumblr serve an adult book club or the Young Adult department best? Information regarding access to mobile devices to operate Tumblr, the organization's goals and practices for social networking, and the Tumblr account's security settings as well as a broad concept of what content will be posted to Tumblr should be established.

For purposes of this instruction, an example of how to set up a Tumblr account for a hypothetical library's Young Adult department will be examined. The hypothetical library serves under the name TheMunicipalLib. TheMunicipalLib has assessed the value of connecting with teens through social media and determined that Tumblr should be used to this end.

TheMunicipalLib will share information about library materials, services, and programming on Tumblr while also taking an avant-garde approach to experimental posts and concepts. Some posts will not directly sell a program or booklist. Instead, TheMunicipalLib will work to entice teens through popular memes (a humorous image, video, piece, or text, etc., that is copied, typically with slight variations, and spread virally by Internet users) and thoughtful articles outside of day-to-day library operations. The library's connections (followers) on Tumblr will be invited to share what they are finding online, reading, viewing, or listening to through the mobile social network.

How to Download and Register a Tumblr Account

The free Tumblr app is available for download from major app stores like iTunes and Google Play. Each provider lists information on the app's ratings from users, specifications, and operating system compatibility for mobile devices.

1. Using a mobile device, search for Tumblr in the app store.
2. After the app has downloaded, Tumblr offers two options: Sign Up or Sign In. Select Sign Up.
3. New users are asked to provide an e-mail account, password, and username. TheMunicipalLib uses the same name for all mobile social network accounts to make its digital presence uniform and easier to locate for followers. For example, TheMunicipalLib will use its Gmail account, themunicipallib@gmail.com, to register for a Tumblr account under the username @TheMunicipalLib.
4. Give the appropriate password to be used for the Tumblr account.
5. Tumblr will ask for the new account user's age. According to the Tumblr Terms of Service, no individual under the age of thirteen may use Tumblr Services. In fact, Tumblr's strict policy includes alternative suggestions for social media users under the age of consent: "You have to be at least 13 years old to user Tumblr. We are serious: it's a hard rule, based on U.S. federal and state legislation. 'But I'm, like, 12.9 years old!' you plead. Nope, sorry. If you're younger than 13, don't use Tumblr. Ask your parent for a Playstation 4, or try reading." (Tumblr, Terms and Services, 3. Use of the Services, Eligibility, https://www.tumblr.com/policy/en/terms-of-service, last modified 1/27/2014)
6. Tumblr will ask new users to follow blogs of interest and will showcase popular Tumblr accounts at the time of registration. This step is a great opportunity to follow library Tumblr accounts, accounts of interest, and accounts of patrons, library associations, and authors. Following accounts that can help connect the library to wider audiences and provide timely information on library services generates a repertoire of resources to adapt and share for the library's marketing strategy. Following blogs of interest can be skipped during registration as well and addressed again later.

Navigating the Tumblr Dashboard

Upon registration, the Tumblr dashboard (user interface) will appear. The Tumblr dashboard consists of the account's Tumblr feed (much like a user's Facebook wall) and five buttons on the bottom tray.

These five buttons from left to right are: the Home button, the Search button, the Post button, the Account button, and the Activity button.

Home, an icon of a house, takes users back to their Tumblr feed. A Tumblr feed is a live update of posts shared by the users followed by the Tumblr account.

Search, which is the magnifying glass to the right of the home icon, takes users to a search bar as well as the feed to Trending Topics and Trending Blogs. Trending Topics are akin to Twitter Trends as they are determined by an algorithm that calculates high user interest and posting.

Tumblr is unique in that its searching facets permit users to search multiple words as well as phrases with spacing. While Tumblr does not limit the amount of hashtags attached to posts, only the first five tags from a post are searchable (i.e., show results when searched) by others.

Post, the pencil in the bottom center of the dashboard, takes users to a list of possible posting options: text, photo, quotes, link, chat, and video. The design of each type of post is similar yet subtly altered to distinguish the type of post submitted. Link and quote posts have a thick header. Photo and video remove the default (but optional) title field. This list of options includes a "Nevermind" button in case users do not wish to share content after clicking Post.

Account, the icon of a person, gives users access to their profile and account settings. Within the Profile tab, users can view their likes, who they are following, notifications, and their blogs. For users with multiple Tumblr blogs, the Account tab is where they will toggle between various Tumblr presences. Selecting an individual blog will permit the user to access the profile settings for that blog.

Activity, the lightning bolt icon on the right bottom side of the dashboard, shows likes, reblogs, and new followers. On a user's Tumblr profile page, the blog's activity is tracked like a hospital monitor and will show high and low points of activity with a line graph.

1. Tap each button to navigate the dashboard facts.

2. Scroll left to right to view Trending Topics.
3. Scroll up and down to view Trending Blogs.
4. Tap Settings under the Account tab to access notifications toggle.

The Tumblr app will use pop-ups to share tips with new users. For example, Tumblr shows users how to share appreciation for posts they see with an illustration of the Tumblr heart ("like" button). When Tumblr asks you, "See something you like?" tap the heart to like the post. The person who posted it will get a note that you like his or her stuff.

How to Set Up a Tumblr Profile

Under the Account tab, tap Blogs to access the account's profile settings. A Tumblr account's profile is how other Tumblr members see the account. The profile consists of a header image, an avatar (an icon or figure representing a particular person, business, or brand online), a title, and a description.

1. Click the Account button.
2. Tap the appropriate blog.
3. Select the Edit Appearance button on the upper right side of the interface.

   In Edit Appearance mode each facet of the Tumblr profile can be selected for editing. TheMunicipalLib's Tumblr space is designated to the Young Adult department, teen resources, materials, and services.
4. Tap the header space to update the header color or image.

   TheMunicipalLib's Tumblr header is a photo of the library on a bright, sunny day. The header is easy to change during national library campaigns throughout the year such as Teen Tech Week, Teen Read Week, Banned Books Week, and Choose Privacy Week. New art and information is commissioned each year for library campaigns on a national scale and is designed for advertising and mobile social marketing.
5. Tap the avatar square in the center of the header image to edit the image.

TheMunicipalLib can use book covers for events featuring popular titles or titles that are being made into films. With permission, the library could use a photo of teens at an event to humanize the Tumblr account as well. If the library has a logo, or more specifically a logo for the Young Adult department, it could be used for the avatar to make the library's Tumblr account distinct.

6. Name the Tumblr account by tapping the bold Untitled link.

   TheMunicipalLib's Young Adult department is called the Teen Space. Its Tumblr account is a digital presence to represent the physical space available for teens and young adults at TheMunicipalLib. TheMunicipalLib's Tumblr account is titled Teen Space.

7. Provide a bio or description of TheMunicipalLib's Teen Space Tumblr account by tapping the Description link beneath the account name. Creating a bio for Tumblr is an optional step. Some libraries on Tumblr opt out of sharing additional information and let their posts speak for themselves. Many groups and organizations use their mission statements on their social network bios. Other groups provide a brief description (typically limited to 140 characters) on the services and goods they provide.

   TheMunicipalLib describes its Teen Space and introduces the contributing librarians to the Tumblr account by tagging them: "Teen Space is the place to be for the newest downloads and books. Check out our amazing events. Posts by @SHelmick and @APilky."

   The accent and background colors can be altered from the Edit Appearance facet on the account's profile. Everything posted and reblogged will show up on the Tumblr's feed in these colors.

8. Tap Save on the right upper corner to save the edits to the Tumblr account's appearance. Tap Cancel to disregard changes and keep the account's previous appearance settings.

How to Post a GIF to a Teen-Themed Tumblr

TheMunicipalLib's introductory post for its Teen Space Tumblr will start the tone of interaction with its followers. A quote post about books or reading holds the weight of a meaningful thought shared about a primary goal of the Teen Space. A text post announcing the Teen Space's presence to Tumblr has an element of official dialogue. TheM-

Figure 5.1. Navigating the Tumblr Dashboard.

unicipalLib wishes to hit the ground running and to share content that is complementary to the Tumblr platform rather than repeating traditional marketing found on TheMunicipalLib's Facebook account.

1. Create or select an appropriate GIF and save it in the mobile device's camera roll.

   Several GIF generators can be found online including gifmaker.me and makeagif.com. Open-source GIF repositories online are growing in popularity and diversity. Sharing GIFs created by others from sites like giphy.com gives the library the opportunity to promote citation through social media and furnishes sources for its followers to explore. Tagging GIF Tumblr posts with their origin encourages further inspection of the information and is known as good "Tumblr etiquette."

TheMunicipalLib's first post is an "Okay." GIF from the young adult novel, *The Fault in Our Stars.* John Green's book and the subsequent film adaptation has reached massive commercial popularity. The library's use of this GIF capitalized on the momentum of the acclaim of *The Fault in Our Stars* while advertising an upcoming program at the Teen Space.

2. Tap the Post button.
3. Choose a format for the post: text, photo(s), quote, link, chat, or video. To post a GIF, select Text Post.

   Note that a text post will share a body of text, while a chat post will structure a text conversation to post between Tumblr users in the design of "Speaker 1 said: This" and "Speaker 2 said: That." Videos and photos visually engage an audience as they give followers a broader perspective shared by the library rather than a single concept presented by the library. A link or quote similarly provides an outside view appreciated by the library and complementary to library praxis.
4. Upload the GIF from the camera roll onto Tumblr.

   Once the Photo Post button has been selected, the mobile device's camera roll will permit users to select up to ten images to post.
5. Select Next on the upper right corner of the dashboard.
6. Add a caption to the post.

   TheMunicipalLib shares information on the *Fault in Our Stars* viewing party for teens in the post's caption. "See the film. Eat some snacks. Make and take crafts. Friday @ 6:30pm."
7. Tap the sales tag icon beneath the caption to tag the post.

   TheMunicipalLib will tag the book and author and create a tag called "Teen Space" to begin a heading to search for its Tumblr posts in the future. Typing the title "Fault in Our Stars" into the tag fields will prompt suggestions for tags by Tumblr. Choosing the popular format of the suggested tag "#thefaultinourstars" increases the post's searchability. Typing "John Green" prompts the tag "#johngreen." TheMunicipalLib adds "#teenspace" as the final tag.

Other Tumblr users can be tagged within posts.

8. If applicable, tap the @ symbol on the right of the tagging field. Choose the appropriate Tumblr connection(s) to tag in the post and separate their names with a space.
9. Select Post on the upper right corner of the dashboard. Upon clicking Post, TheMunicipalLib's status update can be seen under the tags "#thefaultinourstars," "#johngreen," and "#teen-space" together or individually. While millions of posts will be found under the tag "#thefaultinourstars," searching "the fault in our stars + teen space" should limit the search enough to easily find TheMunicipalLib's post.

The new Tumblr post will automatically show up on the Tumblr's profile and on the feed of all the follows of the Tumblr account. From the profile or account feed, posts can be shared to other social networks using the Share button on the lower left side of each update.

How to Respond and Reblog on Tumblr

Tumblr posts give users three options:

1. Share is a square icon with an arrow pointing up through the top. Tap this button to share the post to social networks registered on the mobile device, as an e-mail, or as an SMS (short message service or text).
2. Reblog is an icon consisting of two arrows, one pointing right and one pointing left. Reblog allows users to place posts they like on their own Tumblr feed. A Tumblr account holder reblogging a post is similar to a Facebook user sharing a status update to his or her own wall or a Twitter user retweeting a tweet from another person's Twitter feed.
3. Heart is a heart-shaped icon that is applied to show that a post is liked.

   Tumblr users will show appreciation and support for others' posts by hearting (liking) or reblogging them. While Tumblr users will be notified of all activity for their posts, posts will only spread beyond their personal Tumblr feed when other members of the mobile social network reblog their content.

Figure 5.2. Posting to Tumblr.

Reblogging boosts posts among Tumblr walls with direct and indirect relationships and connects followers to followers. All the followers of a Tumblr feed will see who can be originally attributed to a post. In fact, reblogging a post that is already a reblog will still break down the outreach of the post until it displays the original poster.

1. Select a post to reblog.
2. Tap the Reblog button beneath the post that is to be shared.
3. Add a caption (if desired) to the post.
4. Tap the tagging field to tag a search term or another Tumblr account to the reblog.

How to Search and Create Tags on Tumblr

Tumblr has the capability to allow its users to search multiple hashtags simultaneously. For example, a librarian could search #library and #throwbackthursday to see what other libraries are posting to their followers. Tumblr posts can have unlimited tags; however, only the first five tags on a post are searchable.

Tap the sales tag icon on the bottom left side of a post to add tags. Tags can be easily created and separated with commas. Tap the @ symbol on the right bottom side of a post to add mentions to other Tumblr users.

HOW TO USE SNAPCHAT FOR LIBRARY SOCIAL MEDIA MARKETING

Librarians can enjoy and exploit the intimacy of private, instant chatting with users through Snapchat. With the advent of digital collections and resources available through library websites, content has existed in a patron's pocket for nearly a decade. Connection, however, exists for the first time as libraries employ mobile social marketing to engage on a personal level.

The unique, brief conversations on Snapchat can take the form of ten-second public service announcements for upcoming programs, reader's advisory down to the specific patron, or a touchstone advertisement to remind users of available services. Snap a photo or a quick video to share the library's narrative to a significant group of users on their own turf.

Snapchat's features offer a variety of library marketing opportunities. Upon registering for a Snapchat account, Snapchat Support allows users to search through FAQs, watch how-to tutorials, and edit account settings. Simple instructions for creating and sending snaps as well as contributing a snap to My Story are at your fingertips. My Story is part of a Snapchat profile that enables Snapchat friends a twenty-four-hour window to view and share a single snap through the application. In June 2014, the success of My Story was expanded for public, group-sharing snaps, called Our Story, to connect using geolocation during concerts and major events.

Many librarians choose to add snaps on the My Story option for their library Snapchat because this type of snap allows everyone to view it for a twenty-four-hour period as many times as they wish. The longevity of My Story snaps allows librarians to create daily contests or scavenger hunts that users can refer to on multiple occasions.

Getting Started

Before completing the registration for a Snapchat account, building a Snapchat marketing plan that adheres to a library's marketing policies and procedures is essential. Information regarding access to mobile devices to operate Snapchat, the organization's goals and practices for social networking, and the Snapchat account's security settings as well as a general concept of what content will be posted should be determined.

In the app's infancy, Snapchat users were required to link their account with a phone number to increase social discoverability among mutual contacts. Due to security abuses of the API (application programming interface), members of Snapchat can opt out of using a phone number to create an account. This update may be favorable for libraries that do not have a main phone line that is popular enough to be saved in the devices of their patrons. This update may not be favorable for librarians who can utilize their social network capital to bring users to their library's mobile presences. A balance between creating the widest reach possible and preserving a secure network must be set by the individual organization.

For the purposes of this instruction, an example of how to create a campaign involving "Saturday Shelfies" will be explored. The hypothetical library operates under the name TheMunicipalLib and desires to increase awareness of the library's operational hours and services on Saturdays. Librarians and library users will be asked to share what they are perusing during Saturdays at the library and to pose for a selfie in front of a shelf of books—a "shelfie." TheMunicipalLib's connections through Snapchat will be invited to share what they are reading, viewing, or listening to through the mobile social venue.

How to Download and Register a Snapchat Account

The free Snapchat app is available for download from major app stores like iTunes and Google Play. Each provider lists information on the app's software compatibility, ratings from users, and specifications. Snapchat images and videos can be used to post updates to other social media networks like Twitter, Instagram, and Vine, however, Snapchat does not integrate content to other networks. To create a Snap, register for an account, give the application permission to connect to the devices' contacts or elect to input contacts into the account, tap the circle in the center, bottom of the screen, and hold down to record. Snaps can record up to ten seconds of video.

1. Using a mobile device, search for Snapchat in the app store. Download the Snapchat app to the device.
2. After the app has downloaded, the Snapchat home screen allows users to log in and to sign up. Tap Sign Up.
3. Enter an e-mail address, password, and date of birth, then tap Sign Up again. Create a username, which will be your unique identity on Snapchat, and tap Continue. It is not currently possible to change the username for an existing Snapchat account. TheMunicipalLib uses the same name for all mobile social network accounts to make its digital presence uniform and easier to locate for users.
4. Decide if the new account will use a phone number for users to find the account. Designating a phone number for a Snapchat account should be approached as discriminately as the e-mail and account name. The choice to grant potential followers an additional method to discover the library on mobile social media though a phone number is a balance between security and access.

   Snapchat is distinctive in its approach to user accounts. Avatars and bios are not a part of Snapchat's product. Account names of friends and followers are listed in alphabetic order.

   Verify the phone number for the Snapchat account. While Snapchat will not display this number to other Snapchatters, it is required to verify account information and to locate other Snapchatters in your device's contact list. Snapchat will ask for a second verification by having you select all images containing the Snapchat ghost mascot.

5. Fill in the appropriate password to be used for the Snapchat account.
6. Allow Snapchat to access the device's contacts. Contacts on the device that are using Snapchat will automatically generate into a list of friends for the new account.

   Add other users by names or phone numbers that are not saved on the device used to create the Snapchat account. Team Snapchat is the official account for the team of Snapchat developers and is set as a default friend for all Snapchat accounts. Retaining Team Snapchat as a friend for TheMunicipalLib's Snapchat account will give the library access to notification Snaps, update messages from the developers, and Snapchat news.

Using Snapchat

A professional-looking Snap will require forethought. Snapchat permits text and basic paint overlays on the feed; however, text is limited to thirty-one characters. Mobile devices typically do not permit the sheen of higher-end filming equipment, therefore location, lighting, and sound are elements to take into consideration.

The unique quality of Snapchat in comparison to other mobile social marketing platforms is its original intent to be used as a personal, disposable, controlled method of visual messaging. Tagging is not essential to marketing on Snapchat as snaps are not open to searches nor do they last longer than their play time for recipients.

Snapchat marketing can be approached like other photo messaging campaigns and should include memorable branding and a clear idea. Library mobile marketing with Snapchat ranges from basic instruction and behind-the-scenes peeks to abbreviated collection tours and book recommendations.

Snapchat is relatively new territory to library marketing. Researching existing marketing techniques on Snapchat is also difficult to ascertain because Snapchat communication starts smaller and is done privately through devices rather than on public forums like Facebook or Twitter.

Examine how nonprofits and corporations utilize Snapchat to communicate products and services. Snapchatters have forged creative thoroughfares into their mobile social platform, but Snapchat has much more innovative engagement to offer as it continues to grow. TheMunicipalLib's place in the Snapchat world is dependent on the library's user community.

Between researching the capabilities of a library Snapchat account and submitting that first snap, TheMunicipalLib must complete some housekeeping. Learning how to use Snapchat's various features will give TheMunicipalLib's snaps a clear, more engaging message.

Navigating the Snapchat Dashboard

Navigating the Snapchat dashboard is the first step to creating meaningful snaps for mobile social library marketing. Snapchat's recording interface is composed of five buttons: lighting, camera flip, notification number, record, and a friends list.

Snapchat's intuitive interface makes it possible to explore its facets and begin snapchatting with ease. Before committing to send a snap, play with the drawing, caption, and sharing features. Consider the opportunities for drawing on video and how those opportunities tie into the existing marketing narrative of an organization.

Hold down the Record button and test how long it takes to share information through this medium. Carry around the device with the camera turned on to gain an appreciation for aesthetic views of the library's service space.

From Selfie to Shelfie

The term "selfie" came into its own in the early 2010s. While photographs of social account owners have been common since the heyday of Myspace, there was an observable formality in self-portraits on social networks like Facebook, Twitter, and Flickr. With the onset of image-based mobile photo applications such as ItisMee and Instagram, social networks began to incorporate more amateur, off-the-cuff images of users.

By 2012, "selfie" gained such notoriety on social networks to become one of *Time* magazine's "Top 10 Buzzwords" of the year. Smartphones and mobile devices developed to meet the demand for selfies by adding features like camera inversion, double cameras, and various flash options.

Figure 5.3. How to Navigate Snapchat.

In 2013, the word "selfie" was deemed the "Word of the Year" by the *Oxford English Dictionary*. Selfies have taken place underwater, on every continent on the planet, and in space. The music video from the electric dance music song "#SELFIE" by the Chainsmokers was a viral success online throughout 2014. Selfies are considered to be meme, meta, and material to typical mobile social networking interaction and marketing. Although selfies are here to stay for the foreseeable future of social networking, like most popular phenomena, this mode of graphic communication can be met with much weariness and derision as its popularity plays out.

The following popular craze called "shelfies" was brought about through Instagram by popular photographers, avid readers, and librarians. January 29, 2014, was Instagram's first annual #libraryshelfieday. Over sixty thousand Instagram posts have been tagged with #shelfie, #libraryshelfie, or #libraryshelfieday.

Libraries can use shelfies to promote new materials, special collections, and recently returned items. Asking users to take shelfies of their home library or their favorite section of the library is an interactive method to share an appreciation of reading and promote library access to a wider audience than the library's core followers.

How to Create a Snapchat Shelfie

1. Locate a provocative image of the library space or of library services to photograph or film.
2. Stage an engaging scene. TheMunicipalLib has asked a staff member to hold up a book she is currently reading for a concise Snapchat video. The staff member holds up a book in front of a library display.
3. Tap the red circle in the bottom center of the dashboard. Tapping the circle will take a photo. Holding down the circle will record a video, including sound, as long as one to ten seconds long. TheMunicipalLib staff member holds up the book and says, "Share your shelfies!"
4. Review the snap to determine if it usable for marketing.

   If the snap is out of focus or does not adequately depict the message you wish to convey, simply tap the white X in the upper left corner of the interface. Retry the snap until it is ready to share.
5. Touch the drawing icon on the upper right side of the dashboard and drag a finger across the color palette to find the appropriate color. TheMunicipalLib chooses a bright color to write "Open until 5."

   A message written over the snap is designed to be short and sweet, as it lies over the video or the image. The library has conveyed that it is open on Saturday and ready for business while asking users to share what they are reading and contribute content to the library's digital existence.

6. Using a finger, draw over the image of the snap. Choose several options from the drawing palette to create a colorful message.

   Tap the back arrow icon beside the drawing icon to erase a mistake. The back arrow icon will change colors as the drawing palette uses different colors and will track each movement as an individual pen stroke. By lifting a finger or stylus for the touch screen, the script is saved as a singular piece of writing. For example, a finger can draw the letter J and lift up from the touch screen before adding the title, and both parts of the writing are separately saved.
7. Tap anywhere on the snap to add a caption. The device's keyboard will appear to type a caption for the Snap. TheMunicipalLib can reiterate the messages from the library staff member by typing "Share your shelfies!"
8. Click the arrow pointing right on the bottom right corner of the screen. The list of the account's Snapchat friends will appear with the option to send to a single or multiple users.
9. Select users to send the snap to and tap the arrow bar on the bottom on the interface.

How to Offer Basic Instruction with Snapchat

Snapchat is a fun and engaging means to sneak basic library instruction to users. Rather than waiting for an opportune moment during a reference transaction, proactively demonstrate library resources with quick snaps. These ten-second messages can advertise lesser-known library features and confirm how accessible information can be for patrons.

Consider the frequently asked questions from your community of library users to draw from when creating basic instructional snaps. Ten seconds can quickly inform users how to sign into their online accounts, make a database search, or select an e-book.

Unlike Vine or Instagram, Snapchat does not have a Pause Recording option. The most successful snaps may involve practicing the pitch before filming. To save time, start a snap with action. For example, begin a snap with typing a library card number to sign in while talking about the topic of the snap. Although the length of a snap will not permit you to demonstrate all the facets of a book or article search, distinguishing a feature such as "only show my available titles" starts a

Figure 5.4. Creating a Snap.

meaningful conversation on searching, limiters, and making the library patron's life easier.

How to Give a Behind-the-Scenes Peek

Showcasing behind-the-scenes work and transparency of services is ideal marketing for libraries. Information technology is a broad umbrella term for the daily, weekly, and special skills and activities library professionals employ to serve their community. It is important to educate users, decision makers, and a library's tax base on the scope of library outreach, access, and influence.

Behind-the-scenes snaps can be a storytelling series about library processes. Create a snap juxtaposing the before-and-after process of book preservation. Lay out the tools, line up the staff, and find a book that needs to be preserved to compare to a preserved tome. A visual message on the extent of knowledge, equipment, and labor required to restore a single book provides a clear statement about libraries at work behind closed doors.

Showing prizes for an upcoming reading program whets an audience's appetite, advertises the program, and allows users to learn a behind-the-scenes aspect of building a library program. Snaps can be uncomplicated. Snap the library's side of a return slot as a book comes back, show how a book is checked in, or display staff areas to supply a behind-the-scenes glimpse to Snapchat connections.

How to Showcase New Arrivals

Studies have shown that millennials buy more books than any other demographic. Many of today's library users grew up during the innovations of a rising Amazon.com and its ten-dollar paperback that revolutionized the book market. Making patrons cognizant of popular materials available at their library for free is a highly competitive business. Underestimating the power of word of mouth costs libraries circulation.

Snapchat is an excellent tool to showcase new library materials and recently returned items in the collection. A snap of ten books from the *New York Times* Best Seller list before taking the materials to the library floor or library hold shelf engages users and potential users by sharing what the library has for them. Accessing Snapchat to send out a picture message of recently returned items is another quick way to keep the library's collection in the minds of your followers.

Using Snapchat to present library exhibits and displays can encourage a brand-new audience to visit the brick-and-mortar institution, visit the library website, and sign up for a library card. As library services increasingly become mobile, librarians are finding mobile social platforms to place relevant service information into the hands of potential customers.

How to Recommend a Book

Although it is said to never judge a book by its cover, research suggests up to 73 percent of checkout in a popular collection library is from browsing. Recommending books through a library Snapchat account can bolster checkout and expand reader's advisory.

Snapchat allows users to add text that can be used to describe the book, rate a book, or share the name of a staff member for a staff picks snap. While hashtags cannot be searched on Snapchat, the use of hashtags is a tool to create a dialogue with an audience.

For example, #7wordbooktalk or #7wordbooksynopsis would permit most users the allotted characters required to describe a title in a concise but creative manner. The confines of a seven-word book synopsis challenges staff and users alike to connect about literature and share their skills to articulate. A few of #7wordbooksynopsis for classics include: "Sticks and stones will break your bones" for *The Lottery* by Shirley Jackson, "She kinda made an 'A' of herself" for *The Scarlet Letter* by Nathaniel Hawthorne, "How I Met (and Beheaded) Your Mother" for *Beowulf*, and "Overlook Hotel has five stars on YELP!" for Stephen King's *The Shining*.

Text abbreviations are commonly used on mobile social media marketing but may depend on a library's policy on social media content. Tagging content on Snapchat even though the platform does not use tagging at this time increases the chance for dialogue for the tag on other mobile social networks.

How to Snapchat a Library Contest

The momentum of social media contests helps spread social media marketing of library services and programming. Snapchat contests could include a ten-second book review snap entered to the library's Snapchat account for a random prize drawing, a book scene re-creation snap, or book quote snaps. The University of Mary Hardin–Baylor tailored its Snapchat contest to meet the theme of the 2014 National Library Week theme, "Lives Change @ the Library" as it asked users to make a snap describing a book that changed their worldview.

Using Snapchat to emulate other popular apps can appeal to an audience and feed into trending mobile social applications. Create a snap featuring a book cover, its title, and the question, "Hot or Not?" which is reminiscent of the well-liked matchmaking search engine to capture the impetus of ranking titles in the library's collection.

Snapchat contests require three basic steps for participants. Add the library as a friend on Snapchat, create a snap within the library guidelines, and submit the snap by the library contest due date. A library Snapchat contest can appeal to tweens, teens, and young adults and could be used as a mini assignment for adults taking social media classes at the library.

How to Make an Abbreviated Library Tour

Promoting in-house collections is a valuable application of mobile social marketing platforms for libraries. The ability to economically and efficiently place noncirculating materials into the view of a library's social media followers allows collections to live and thrive. Abbreviated library tours can be created using Snapchat, which will grant users special access to materials that never leave the physical library.

Planning ahead is crucial to exhibit the collection in the strongest way possible when using Snapchat. Select vibrant and interesting articles and items to photograph for a snap. Remember to source the library or the specific collection in the snap so users can explore the materials more in depth at a later date.

Launch a library Snapchat account by sharing the street address of the library, the library's outdoor signage, the library building, or a clip entering through the library's front doors to convey a welcoming atmosphere to Snapchat recipients.

How to Introduce Library Staff

An advantage of mobile social library marketing is the personal voice and interaction afforded through multiple applications. Once a mode of declaration and the intended audience of a library's Snapchat account has been established, snapping introductions of library staff can prove useful in an attempt to humanize and connect with potential users.

Snapchat can be used to ask staff members a question or simply show them in their work environment within the library's complex.

Library staff can hold up their favorite book in a snap or tell recipients their favorite part of working at the library.

As new volunteers and staff enter the fold, they can be acquainted with the library's Snapchat friends with initiatory snaps. Humanizing the information technology revolution is one of the many challenges facing modern librarians. Snapchat is a tool that can assist information specialists in their work to forge interpersonal touchstones with patrons by means of mobile social marketing applications.

How to Promote Security and Privacy

The validity of throwaway online information had been debated long before the arrival of Snapchat. However, this mobile social marketing platform holds a claim to fame for its unique disposable content creation and exchange. The ephemeral aspect of snaps is conversational fodder for information specialists and privacy advocates, and it should be addressed during library classes and interactions.

Classes and handouts on Internet safety and awareness can use Snapchat to teach the digital literacy lesson that the Internet never forgets. Self-destructing content is never guaranteed with online social marketing platforms as tech experts proved with some Snapchat jailbreaking, the process of removing limitation on operating systems, applications, and hardware, as early as December 2013. In January 2014, Snapchat was hacked and more than 4.6 million users had their compromised information published online.

Librarians are responsible to educate consumers on mobile social media platforms and to convey the risks to privacy and autonomy that users may trade in order to use certain applications. Library tech classes, LibGuides, and handouts should cover how-to steps, typical practices, and discussion on privacy and complimentary apps that can change the basic premises of popular mobile social programs.

HOW TO PROVIDE READER'S ADVISORY THROUGH INSTAGRAM

Instagram is gaining ground as one of the most used mobile social marketing applications for libraries. Library Instagram accounts are utilized by public, academic, school, private, and even presidential libraries. Instagram is a searchable mobile social platform that allows participants to explore usernames and hashtags. Hashtags are homogenous to access points or keyword terms in a library catalog and allow users to find photos and videos on a variety of topics stored on the mobile social network's servers.

Instagram's prominence as one of the most popular social media apps is due in part to its ergonomic see, click, and send methodology to photo sharing. With nineteen original filters and perfunctory photo effects, Instagram has grown from a thirteen-employee social network presence to a billion-dollar Facebook acquisition.

In fact, Facebook permits its users to register for Instagram by signing up through their Facebook account. Users may also create an Instagram profile with their e-mail address. Upon registering for an Instagram account, Instagram Help shows users how to edit profile information such as name, username, and contact information, how to become familiarized with Instagram tabs and search functions, and how to create and share photos with step-by-step guides.

Many libraries connect their Instagram account to their Twitter, Facebook, and Tumblr presences to streamline social marketing messages across all the library's platforms. Instagram is available on Android, Apple, and Chrome OS devices and operates similarly on all systems. To create an Instagram account, register for an account, take a photo by tapping the blue circle in the lower center of the screen, swipe to the left to choose an appropriate filter; then select Next to write a caption, tag people, add the picture to Instagram's Photo Map, and share.

Instagram's searchability, strong membership, and facile interface are characteristics that make it a robust mobile social marketing application for librarians to use. Instagram marketing is visual and can be applied like other graphically based campaigns. Clever images, appealing ideas, and captivating tagging are pivotal for successful library Instagram marketing.

Create a Plan

Before registering for an official Instagram account, a few elements should be considered. Mobile social marketing aspects such as access to mobile equipment to use the app, an organization's policies and procedures on mobile social networking, the Instagram account's security settings, the organization's online brand, and a general concept of what will be posted should be assessed.

For the purposes of this instruction, examples of how to create a reader's advisory post and a #WhatAreYouReading Contest post will be fleshed out. The hypothetical library for this instruction operates under the name TheMunicipalLib. Users will have the ability to access the Instagram posts to learn about new nonfiction titles available at the library and to make a contribution to the #WhatAreYouReading contest.

How to Download and Register an Instagram Account

1. Using a mobile device, search for Instagram in the app store. Instagram is a popular application available through iTunes and Google Play.
2. Once the app has downloaded, tap Sign Up or Log In with Facebook. If the organization already possesses a Facebook account, it may be prudent to use Facebook to create the Instagram account, which will automatically sync Instagram posts to the Facebook wall or timeline.

   Designating which e-mail address is used for an Instagram account should be handled as discriminately as selections made for other mobile social networks representing the organization, or which e-mail address is given to media outlets such as radio, television, and newspapers.
3. Provide a name for the Instagram account. The hypothetical library for this instruction operates a Twitter account under the name @TheMunicipalLib and has chosen to keep the brand cohesive with the name TheMunicipalLib.
4. Create a password.
5. Confirm that the e-mail address entered is correct.
6. Add an optional full name, for example, The Municipal Library, and an optional phone number to make it easy for friends and followers of the library to find the new account on Instagram.
7. Follow people, places, and organizations connected to the library service community to see their photos and videos. Instagram can

access Facebook friends as well as the contacts on the mobile device. It can also be mined to find current and potential Instagram connections.

How to Complete an Instagram Profile

1. Tap the profile icon on the bottom right corner of the dashboard.
2. Select Edit Your Profile to edit username and the account's e-mail address or to add a website and a bio. Making Instagram posts private is a setting found under this profile facet.
3. Set a profile photo for the Instagram account. TheMunicipalLib keeps its profile images uniform and uses four photographs of the library building that are updated seasonally as well as a few promotional images provided during major events or national library campaigns.

   The profile picture circle icon in the upper right corner of the profile facet gives users multiple options. They can import a photo from Facebook or Twitter to use as an Instagram profile image. Users can take a photo or choose a photo from the mobile device's camera roll. Users can remove and replace the current photo from this location in the app as well.
4. Confirm the e-mail address and username chosen for the Instagram account.
5. Add the website for the organization being represented with the Instagram account. TheMunicipalLib example uses its library web address to give users another access point to its digital resources through Instagram.
6. Add a bio for the organization's mobile social network presence on Instagram. Many organizations use their mission statements on their social network bios. Other groups provide a brief description (typically limited to 140 characters) on the services and goods they provide.

   TheMunicipalLib describes its physical space in its bio and introduces the contributing librarians to the Instagram account by tagging them: "A haven for the insatiably curious, boasting more than half a million books, epic programs, limitless resources, and friendly staff. Posts by @SHelmick and @APilky."

> Mobile social network bios can be uniform throughout all mobile social network channels or tailored to address the interests and needs of users on a specific platform. For example, "Boasting more than half a million books, movies, and more. Great events, classes, programs, and people. Comfy couches. Free membership. Posts by your friendly librarians, @SHelmick and @APilky."

The rapid-fire exchange associated with Instagram challenges the application of fully visualized and planned-out posts. Instagram is designed for amateurs and professional photographers alike to tell a story with a picture and draw their audience into the worlds loading before them on their feed.

However, policies and procedures can help to preemptively determine an organization's message to its followers. For example, academic libraries may focus on posts showcasing items in the special collection, library resources, and freebies during finals week or introductions featuring library staff and volunteers for new students. Public libraries may focus on new and popular materials, live posts from weekly story times and senior events, or for displaying reading program prizes.

TheMunicipalLib's strategy is to utilize Instagram for reader's advisory and eventually working up to a #WhatAreYouReading Instagram contest.

How to Create and Post Reader's Advisory Instagram Posts

1. Choose how to approach the visual execution of reader's advisory. Select a stack of teen or staff picks, a series from a popular author, new arrivals to the library, or a favorite tome.
2. Stage the material in a captivating manner. Take advantage of the cover page. Consider showing the library's markings and call number on the book. Perhaps the book is a tearjerker and rests next to a box of tissues. Perhaps the photo is a collection of cookbooks stacked next to kitchen utensils.

   TheMunicipalLib example is offering reader's advisory and creating an opportunity for interaction by asking #WhatAreYouReading. TheMunicipalLib staff pose with books they are reading and ask their Instagram audience to share what they are currently reading.

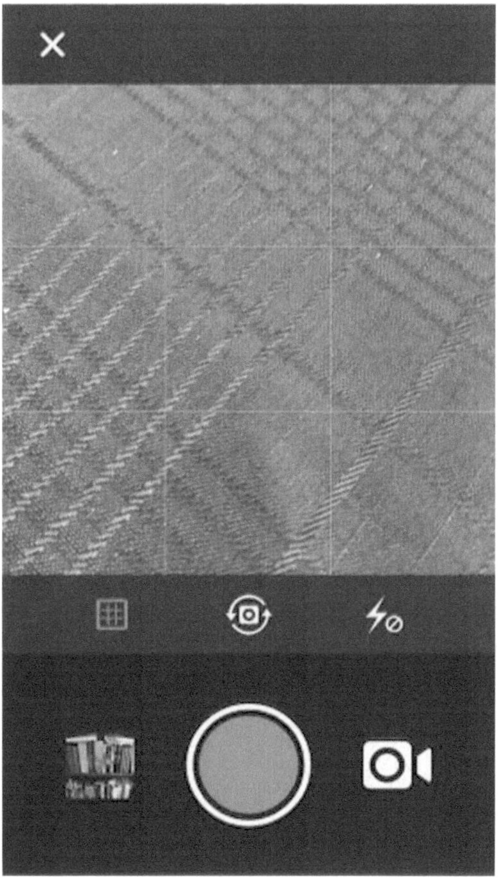

Figure 5.5. Instagram's Camera Interface.

3. Open the Instagram app.
4. Select the Share tab which is the square bottom in the bottom center of the dashboard. The Share tab enables users to snap photos or select pictures from a device's photo albums to use for posts.
5. Tap the blue circle to take a photo. The photo is a TheMunicipal-Lib staff member holding a book that is in TheMunicipalLib collection and is available for checkout.
6. Choose a filter. While Instagram posts do not require a filter, the nineteen colorful options are one of the mobile social network's original claim to fame and can spark interest from viewers.

7. Select Next.
8. Enter a caption. For example, "Adrian is reading Rebecca by Daphne du Maurier." Include hashtags so Instagram users have a greater chance of searching and discovering posts. For example, "Adrian is reading Rebecca by Daphne du Maurier. #WhatAreYouReading?"
9. Tag users if applicable. If Adrian has an Instagram account, it could prove fruitful to tag Adrian's account in order to increase reach by sharing the post with Adrian's friends as well as TheMunicipalLib's followers.
10. Click Share. The post will automatically appear on TheMunicipalLib's dashboard and on the feed of all of TheMunicipalLib's followers.

Users of Instagram can search for other users or content as well as like and comment on shared content. Instagram permits integration of shared content on a variety of social networking platforms, such as Facebook, Twitter, and Tumblr.

Librarians understand the value of judging a book by its cover as well as the adage "A picture is worth a thousand words." Photographs taken during the height of summer reading or during day-to-day operations can sell the benefits of the library in ways a board report cannot. Allowing pictures to tell the library's narrative can be quick, seamless, and far reaching through the use of a library Instagram account.

Instagram Follow-Up

The staff responsible for creating content for TheMunicipalLib's Instagram account will need to follow up on Instagram comments, likes, and shares. Shares to other mobile social platforms such as Twitter and Facebook can be tracked and may compound the reach of a post. A notable advantage of mobile social marketing is the ability to collect data on its reach. Maintaining a record of mobile social marketing impact permits professionals to determine the best courses of action as well as the return on investment for mobile social marketing.

1. Tap below comments to respond.
2. Add additional hashtags to the conversation as applicable.

3. Keep responses limited to 140 characters when possible to maintain a clean, clarion social network presence.
4. Remember to refer to other options of contact such as a library phone number or e-mail address to encourage deeper, reference interactions.

HOW TO USE INSTAGRAM FOR LIBRARY MARKETING

How to Tag on Instagram

Tagging is performed the same way on Instagram, Twitter, Facebook, Tumblr, and Vine. The pound sign, which is also called a hashtag, is placed before the keyword or key phrase desired. The # symbol marks relevant keywords or key phrases to be searched by others. Libraries have been using popular hashtags like #literarymarchmadness, #throwbackthursdays, and #libraryprobz to appeal to their followers.

Librarians can get a glimpse of user behaviors and activities by searching #libraryprobz Instagram results, which are supplied by professionals and patrons alike. This enriched and personalized data can yield insight into how users perceive the library space and its services and lend itself to customized mobile social marketing exchanges. Samples of #libraryprobz include pictures and video of library copier mishaps, students physically camped out in computer labs during finals weeks, and delightful ephemera discovered in returned books.

Sharing the history and impact of a library can be readily marketed with hashtags like #throwbackthursdays. Locating photos from the local history files, newspaper articles from past summer reading programs, and documents describing the past practice and evolution of library services are visual aids that demonstrate the library's continued growth and vitality.

How to Promote Programs

Instagram pictures of program setup and promotional flyers may encourage turnout while live photos of the event keep library users who do not attend updated on what the library is offering to its community.

Instagram is a useful tool for same-time promotion on live library events. During lectures, musical performances, and story times, Instagram can furnish followers with immediate news to make them feel included. Keeping a library's tax base, student body, or alumni groups informed about ongoing programs can help support sustainability and funding efforts.

Instagram videos last from three to fifteen seconds and can be filmed in segments. Captured moments of a library concert or a Teen Advisory Board meeting can be pieced together to form a cohesive representation. Switch from the default photo setting to record an Instagram by selecting the Share button in the bottom center on the interface and sliding the blue circle to the left, which accesses the red recording circle.

Tap the red recording circle to record. Tap the red recording circle again to pause or stop recording. Rapid taps coupled with slight angle changes can create the illusion of a stop-motion video. Stop-motion is an animation technique that physically manipulates an image or object to appear to be moving on its own. A basic library craft project from a children's event can come to life in a short Instagram video for hundreds of followers to see.

How to Transform Printed Marketing into Mobile Marketing

Instagram has actively sought to encourage and monitor digital marketing on the mobile social networking platform. Instagram has implemented a Sponsor label to identify approved ads that stay true to the spirit of the Instagram community as well as a "Hide" button to allow users to remove or provide feedback on ads.

Marketing is an investment of money, time, and resources. In addition, mobile social marketing platforms are part of a modern library's strategic marketing plan and are a proactive measure to ensure that the investment of marketing is as far reaching as possible. Mobile social marketing is comparatively efficient and economical. Library marketing through mobile social networks is an obtainable goal for libraries of all sizes, budgets, and capacities.

Transferring library marketing material into the cloud in order to share it on a library's website and social networks can become procedural. Snapping a picture of the finished product may be quicker and can add a casual quality that can be desired for promotional dialogue. An attractive image that includes the location, times, and dates as appropriate can be uploaded faster on Instagram than it can be printed and placed on a bulletin board.

Research creative library signage and displays from other users on Instagram to determine which styles are working. Libraries are reversing mobile marketing capabilities to create Instagram-themed hardcopy handouts: "If the Character Had Instagram" interactive displays with hashtags to ascribe genres, authors, and titles. Other libraries are producing "30 Day" Instagram challenges to their followers by seeking a book-themed image each day for a month.

HOW TO USE VINE FOR LIBRARY INSTRUCTION

Unlike Instagram, Vine is a completely video-based social media application. The uploaded videos, or "vines," are posts lasting from one to six seconds. Vines are unique for looping continuously on the social profile in comparison to other video posts on Facebook, Snapchat, and Instagram, which play a single time.

Vines can connect to other major social media applications such as Twitter and Facebook, which has aided its growth in becoming a mobile network with over forty million users. Four months after Vine was founded, Twitter purchased the mobile application for $30 million in October 2012. Vine is available for Android, Google Play, and iOS devices.

Make a Plan

Before registering for an official Vine account a few considerations must be made. Information about access to mobile equipment to use Vine, an organization's policies and procedures on mobile social networking, the Vine account's security settings, the organization's online brand, and a general concept of what will be posted should be assessed.

For the purposes of this instruction, an example of how to create a library instructional video on Vine will be explored. The hypothetical library operates under the name TheMunicipalLib. Users will have the ability to access the Vine post to learn how to make a basic search on the library's online card catalog.

The free Vine app can be downloaded from iTunes and Google Play. Each provider offers information on the app software compatibility, user rating, and specifications. Vine publishes its sharing procedures and rating policy, which are congruent with the policies of Apple and Google.

How to Download and Register a Vine Account

To create a Vine account, download the Vine application to your device. The Vine application's home screen allows "Viners" to sign in with Twitter, sign up with an e-mail account, or log in. To connect the library's Twitter account with its new Vine account, select Sign In with Twitter. To register a library Vine account independent of the library's Twitter account, tap Sign Up with Email.

Fill in the required registration information including name, e-mail address, and password. Vine allows its users the option of entering their phone number, contacts list, and Twitter followers to find fellow Viners. Tap the green avatar to update your Vine account's profile image. Choose an image from your device's camera roll or take a new picture. Here are detailed instructions:

1. Using a mobile device, search for Vine in the app store.
2. Once the app has downloaded, select Sign Up with Email or Log In with Twitter. If the organization already possesses a Twitter account, it may be prudent to use Twitter to create the Vine account, which will automatically sync Vine posts to the Twitter timeline.

   Designating which e-mail address is used for a Vine account should be handled as discriminately as selections made for other mobile social networks representing the organization, or which e-mail address is given to media outlets such as radio, television, and newspapers.
3. Provide a name for the Vine account. The hypothetical library already runs Instagram and Twitter accounts under the name @TheMunicipalLib and has chosen to keep the brand cohesive with the name TheMunicipalLib.

4. Set a profile photo for the Vine account. This can be accomplished by using a photo already in the mobile device's camera roll or by taking a picture and selecting it for the profile. TheMunicipalLib keeps its profile images uniform and uses four photographs of the library building that are updated seasonally as well as a few promotional images provided during major events or national library campaigns.
5. Fill in the appropriate e-mail address and password to be used for the Vine account.
6. Select topics of interest. Vine will use these selections to share featured posts to TheMunicipalLib's Vine feed. Topics include art, family, DIY, science and tech, sports, and news.
7. Upload contacts to Vine, if applicable. TheMunicipalLib's contacts for other mobile social networks such as Snapchat, Twitter, and Instagram can be searched by Vine to find existing Viners within the library's current audience.
8. Explore the Vine dashboard, features, and feed, which is also referred to as a timeline.

   Examining the Vine feed of TheMunicipalLib furnishes insight into the interests and colloquialisms of local and current audience members. Studying the work of other library Vine accounts as well as the Vine accounts of successful organizations and companies teaches what works, what doesn't work, and where Vine trends are going.

Rather than reinventing the wheel, it is useful to take stock of Viners' contributions to make an educated appraisal of TheMunicipalLib's spot in the Vine world. Tips and tricks can be gleaned in a manner of moments by taking stock of the most followed libraries on Vine, the most watched or looped videos, and the most engaging content produced as suggested by shares and comments.

Housekeeping

Between research and the first Vine post, housekeeping tasks can be accomplished immediately and efficiently. TheMunicipalLib profile can be completely updated with a few steps:

1. Select the profile figure in the bottom left corner of the dashboard.
2. Tap Settings to access the account, profile, and security settings.
3. Tap A Few Words about Yourself to add a bio for the account. Many organizations use their mission statements on their social network bios. Other groups provide a brief description (typically limited to 140 characters) on the services and goods they provide.

   TheMunicipalLib describes the physical space in its bio and introduces the contributing librarians to the Vine account by tagging them: "A haven for the insatiably curious, boasting more than half a million books, epic programs, limitless resources, and friendly staff. Vines by @SHelmick and @APilky."

   Bios can be verbatim throughout all mobile social network presences or tailored to address the interests and needs of users on a specific platform. For example, "Find books, music, movies, and more in 6 seconds. TheMunicipalLib is your one stop spot for programs, entertainment, and lifelong education. Vines by your friendly librarians, @SHelmick and @APilky."
4. Type in the location of the Vine account. Vine enables users to be creative with their location information. TheMunicipalLib can choose to share what city or state in which it operates, share the physical street address of its main branch, or it can share its website as a location.
5. Choose a profile color from the nine available colors for Vine accounts.
6. Manage the account to suit marketing, security, and notifications needs. Settings gives users access to change the account name, the e-mail, and password and privacy options.
7. Your Content is a unique Settings feature that breaks down the account content into:

   Protected Posts, which only followers can view. Protected posts can tailor vines to specific audiences. For example, weekly teen programs can be vined and promoted frequently for teen followers, who are statistically more likely to be active on Vine, without flooding the feed on passive Viners who may not attend such events.

   Sensitive Posts, for Vine posts containing sensitive content. Some Viners find tagging their content as sensitive useful, as Vine warns potential viewers when a "post may contain sensitive content." Sensitive posting adds a barrier between streaming content to permit viewers the option to click and watch a vine.

Open VM [Vine Messages] Inbox, to permit messages from everyone. To access Vine Messages, tap the speech bubble icon on the upper left corner of the dashboard. Individual names can be tapped to open and continue conversations. To send Vine Messages, tap the speech bubble icon, then the camera icon, record a message, preview the creation to add text, tap Next, then select the recipients to receive the message.

Address Book, to upload and store contacts.

A Deactivate Account option, for users who elect to delete their account.

Once TheMunicipalLib account is managed and prepped for public viewing, vines can be created and posted. The simplicity of vine creation is one of the mobile social network's secret to wide use and popularity.

Since vines are limited to posts from one to six seconds long, planning is essential to communicating information to users. Third-party screencast applications and web recorders help Viners to demonstrate website navigation directly from the site. Recording library volunteers and staff using library resources may humanize the process and present instructional vines as simple and accessible.

TheMunicipalLib desires to create a series of instructional vines to demonstrate how to use the library's services. For its inaugural post, the library will vine a basic online card catalog search for the classic novel *Rebecca* by Daphne du Maurier.

How to Create an Instructional Vine

The brief exchange of information authorized through Vine requires considerable planning before filming and uploading content. Components to consider include (a) the visual finished product, (b) camera stability, (c) creating a perfect loop, and (d) video basics, such as the rule of thirds.

The finished product of a vine should look like a well-lit, thoroughly designed narration. Whether the library is showing users how to use the self-checkout stations or how to find databases on the library's mobile website, the vine used to convey this information should be executed step by carefully considered step.

Deciding to move a camera or keep it stationary is important to the overall production of a vine. Following other Vine accounts or Viners can inspire and teach new users how to use camera angles and movement to boost vines. Other Viners can show the art of the perfect loop. Strong vines will articulate a message and loop back as seamlessly as possible as it replays.

Brushing up on filmography and camera basics will immediately strengthen vines. The rule of thirds is a guideline that applies two equally spaced horizontal and vertical lines over the compositional element being filmed or photographed. This spacing divides an image into nine uniform parts. Aligning the person or thing filmed for a vine within these proportions creates a professional and energetic product.

When you're ready to get started, this is what you'll want to do:

1. Tap the camera icon in the bottom center of the dashboard. Vine asks if a user is new to Vine and offers to walk users through how to make their first post. Vine offers an interactive tour to assist the user with the creation of a Vine post by instructing the user to hold a finger on the screen over what is to be recorded.

   Option A: Record a continuous vine:

   Continuous vines can be a bit tough to master as a new user. However, vines can be recorded as continuous videos or broken down into multiple shots by tapping on the screen of the recording mobile device. An example of a long vine recording would include: navigating the library's website, accessing the online library catalog, typing a title, and clicking Search. Whether the instruction is recorded as a screencast or as an informal demonstration of a staff member's search, Vine records video and sound. Staff could quickly recite the web address for the online catalog or give a brief guide such as, "Visit our site and click My Account."

   Option B: Record a stop-motion vine:

Figure 5.6. Recording a Vine.

An example of a brief succession of shots to offer instruction would include a clear depiction of the library's uniform resource locator (URL), followed by a clip of each tab leading to the online card catalog, then a clip of the search bar with the search typed in it, and finally an image of the search results.

Sharing instruction through Vine can grab a user's attention. When the narrative of Vine instruction is finely tuned, a post will share pertinent information that is simple to digest and comprehend. The stop-motion approach to vines should not overflow with images or concepts. Regulating no more than one idea per second in instructional vines gives the eyes and mind time to adjust to the steps needed to access services.

2. Click the green circular checkmark to submit the recording for sharing.
3. Add a caption describing or enhancing the message of the vine. By adding a popular tag like #books or #library to the caption, users increase their chances of discoverability.
4. Choose a location for the vine.
5. Select a channel. Channels are the topics of interest that were selected during registration. By selecting a channel that relates to

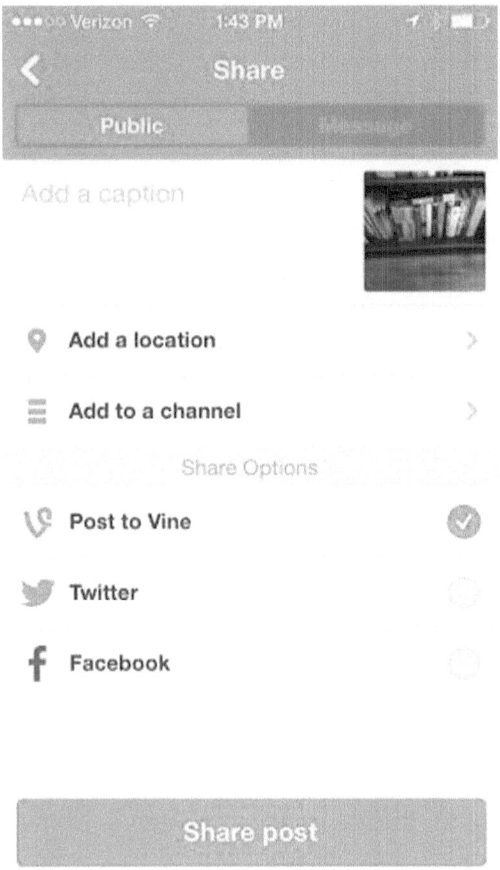

Figure 5.7. Sharing a Vine.

the topic of the vine, users increase their chances of discoverability.

6. Click on Share Options to sync the Vine post with Twitter and Facebook.
7. Click Share.

The new vine immediately uploads to TheMunicipalLib feed once Share has been clicked. The number of views or loops appear in the upper right-hand corner of the vine. Options to like, comment, share, and delete are available below each vine posted.

TheMunicipalLib could produce instructional vines to post on a weekly basis to be shared on its other mobile social networks as well. Vines are a complementary resource to handouts or flyers or step-by-step guides on the library's website.

Vine Follow-Up

The staff responsible for creating content for TheMunicipalLib's Vine account will need to follow up on vine comments as well as track each post's likes, views (loops), and shares. A notable advantage of mobile social marketing is the ability to collect data on its reach. Maintaining a record of mobile social marketing impact permits professionals to determine the best courses of action.

Use Vine for Six-Second Reader's Advisory

Librarians are challenged to meet user needs and to assist users where they are in their community. As social media marketing platforms like Vine become part of the community, librarians adapt their services to fit. Six-second reader's advisory can seem daunting until it's considered to be like an elevator pitch. In an elevator pitch, candidates have considered their strongest points and have practiced selling their marketability in a memorable and appealing manner.

Reader's advisory on Vine is very much like an elevator pitch. Consider a book's strengths and how to grab an audience with an enthralling description, breakdown, or quote that can be recorded and shared with Vine followers. For example, merging #7wordbooksynopsis with Vine could be a fun opportunity for users to record their abbreviated book descriptions through a "Seven Words in 6 Seconds Book Challenge."

HOW TO HOST A LIBRARY CONTEST FOR TWITTER

Millions of Twitter users develop and share information every single day. Followers of small businesses, large companies, not-for-profit groups, charities, universities, celebrities, authors, politicians, and innumerable brands communicate directly with these content creators. Twitter users value official Twitter accounts as a primary point of contact for goods, services, news, and entertainment.

Libraries can take advantage of the popularity of Twitter to promote resources, directly address customer service questions, and generate discussion. Many libraries and library associations utilize Twitter to connect with colleagues and spread information about events, developments, and trends within the realms of library science and information technology.

From a marketing perspective, Twitter provides symmetry between brands and their customers. A librarian can answer a customer's tweet about new books with a quick 140-character reply with similar ease and finesse used by airlines for their customers' tweets about upgrades. The gold standard of mobile social promotion is the maturation of customer-driven content into a memorable marketing campaign. Creating a library Twitter contest is an example of gathering user-driven content for advertising purposes.

Getting Started

Determine how Twitter adheres to and complements a library's marketing policy before creating an account. Assess the library's social marketing policy, guidelines, and best practices. Should the library's Twitter account represent the entire library or focus on specific library departments? Library staff must be knowledgeable and have access to training on mobile devices to operate Twitter. The library's long-range goals for social networking, the Twitter account's security settings, and an outlined concept of potential marketing content to Twitter should be established.

For purposes of this instruction, an example of how to set up a Twitter account for a hypothetical library Twitter contest will be inspected. The hypothetical library serves under the name TheMunicipalLib. TheMunicipalLib has assessed the value of producing user content about library services and determined that Twitter should be used as the medium of the endeavor.

TheMunicipalLib will share information about library resources and events on Twitter beyond the petition for entries for a library contest. Some posts will promote materials and services and provide links to digital collections when possible. The library's Twitter followers will be invited to share how they use their library. Examples of use will be demonstrated by members of library staff as they find information with library databases, participate in a library program, and use the library's multimedia offerings.

How to Download and Register a Twitter Account

The free Twitter app is available for download from major app stores like iTunes and Google Play. Each provider lists information on the app's ratings from users, specifications, and operating system compatibility for mobile devices.

1. Using a mobile device, search for Twitter in the app store.
2. After the app has downloaded, Twitter offers two options: Sign Up or Log In. Select Sign Up.
3. New users are asked to provide an e-mail account or phone number as well as a full name, a username, and a password. TheMunicipalLib uses the same name for all mobile social network accounts to make its digital presence uniform and easier to locate for followers. For example, TheMunicipalLib will use its Gmail account, themunicipallib@gmail.com, to register for a Twitter account under the username @TheMunicipalLib.
4. Give the appropriate password to be used for the Twitter account. Select Sign Up again.
5. Twitter suggests adding a phone number to connect with friends. Use the appropriate phone number to connect the library's official Twitter account with friends and potential followers or skip this step.

6. Twitter will ask for access to the contact list on the device being used to register for the library's Twitter account. Twitter securely uploads contacts to support the new account with suggested Twitter friends and followers. Choose OK to give access to the device's contacts or select Don't Allow to skip this step.
7. Twitter will suggest approximately one hundred accounts to follow. This step is a great opportunity to follow library Twitter accounts and other accounts of interest as well as accounts of patrons, library associations, and authors. Following accounts that can help connect the library to wider audiences and provide timely information on library services is key to a library's outreach marketing strategy. Following other Twitter accounts can be skipped during registration and revisited.

How to Create a Twitter Profile:

Upon registration, Twitter tells users to "encourage people to follow you by sharing something about yourself." A Twitter profile includes a 140-character bio and an avatar (profile photo).

Twitter bios should be thoughtful in their description of a brand's scope of services. Libraries often denote their special collections, mission statement, or commitment to programming. TheMunicipalLib's bio reads, "A haven for the insatiably curious, with more than 2 million books, epic programs, limitless resources and a friendly staff. Tweets by @ASmith and @BJones."

Twitter followers would rather interact with a person than a logo. Adding the Twitter handles of staff members responsible for contributing updates to the library's account drives users to the library Twitter and gives a face to the brand. Twitter bios can include tagging to the library's municipal government, university, or corporation to guide followers to networked accounts.

Build brand recognition and consistency by using the same profile image through all the library's social media accounts. A picture of the physical library space or the library's logo help to make the library's mobile social presence easily recognizable. Once the library's Twitter profile is created, Twitter Settings provide design themes to select or customize for use behind the profile image.

How to Manage Twitter Settings

Tapping the gear icon on the left of Edit Profile gives users access to their Twitter account's Settings (notifications services), Lists (subscriptions of tailored lists used to follow Twitter accounts meeting specific criteria), Help (link to the Twitter Support Center) and Sign Out.

1. Select Settings.
2. Tap the name of the library account.
3. Choose Mobile Notifications. Determine which notifications would behoove the library account managers to receive and slide each option to On or Off as appropriate. Twitter users can receive notifications on a variety of account activities including: retweets, favorites (likes), new followers, direct messages, and mentions.

How to Search in Twitter

Search is the magnifying glass on the upper right corner of the Twitter profile. Tapping the Search button brings up a search bar. Twitter users can search a word, a phrase, or other Twitter accounts with the @ symbol and hashtags (#). Trending topics and accounts can be found by searching the word "trend." Promoted tweets (tweets companies pay Twitter to have pushed to the top of search results) and Twitter trends are determined by an algorithm that calculates high user interest and posting.

1. Tap the search bar.
2. Enter a term or tag to search.
3. Choose Top Tweets to view the highest-ranked tweets about the search term or tag used.
4. Choose All Tweets to view the most current tweets about the term or tag searched as well as all tweets concerning the search.

How to Post a Tweet

Post, the pencil to the right of the Search button, takes users to a dialogue box. TheMunicipalLib will need to promote its library Twitter contest on its official Twitter account. To encourage users to post, the library has developed the hashtag #HowDoYouLibrary to add to posts about using the library's services. Possible media to tweet for this contest are text, GIFs, photos, links, videos, and mentions.

1. Select Post to open the tweet dialogue box.
2. Create a message within the framework of 140 characters. Remember, Twitter requires twenty-two characters for links starting with "http," twenty-three characters for links starting with "https," and twenty-three characters for each photo attachment to a tweet.
3. TheMunicipalLib's first tweet about its library Twitter contest called "#HowDoYouLibrary" says, "#HowDoYouLibrary? Tag & share your library activities to us to be entered in a Show & Tell contest for a Kindle Fire!"
4. Share the Twitter post on the library's other mobile social media accounts to boost its reach. Promotion of the library's Twitter contest should occur on the library's mobile social media accounts, on the library's website, within the library's physical space, and by word of mouth. Retweeting entries into the contest will show appreciation to participants and generate interest. User content gleaned from the contest offers insight into user patterns and behavior and furnishes qualitative data for library stakeholders.

   Library staff must consider the commitment of time and resources to develop a contest, ascertain a winner and possible runners-up for the #HowDoYouLibrary entries, and market on Twitter the contest outcome and related social media events as they happen. Asking customers #HowDoYouLibrary in an interactive contest opens the door to a level conversation. By suggesting patrons should determine how to use library-provided information to enrich their lives, libraries move away from marketing "how to use resources" to "don't miss out on resources" campaigns.

HOW TO CREATE A FACEBOOK GROUP FOR A LIBRARY BOOK CLUB

Libraries exist in a nearly constant state of flux between thriving from the traditional foundations of library services and striving to support digital communities with expanding technology and innovation. As librarians define a balance between seasoned and contemporary service approaches, they draw on mobile social media marketing to combine both. Facebook can help libraries merge the best of both worlds.

Facebook is one of a long list of mobile social networks. While it was not the first social media service on the block, it is ubiquitous among

Figure 5.8. Tagging and Uploading Twitter Pics.

global users of mobile communication. Facebook is the first stop for all brands entering the world of mobile social media marketing. Facebook is so widely known and used that a library Facebook account connects users with services across multiple socioeconomic, cultural, and generational populations.

Getting Started

Methods in which Facebook can be utilized to meet the library's mobile social marketing goals should be determined before creating an account. Library staff must have some mobile social media experience as well as access to training. In the case of Facebook Groups, a personal Facebook account credentials must be used to build a group from which the library can benefit. Staff's knowledge, social media acuity, and professionalism are key to mobile social marketing success.

For purposes of this instruction, an illustration on how to set up a Facebook group for a library's book club will be detailed. The hypothetical library for this project operates under the name TheMunicipalLib. In this example, TheMunicipalLib has hosted a book club for several years and would like to add a social media component to the program. TheMunicipalLib anticipates using the Library's Facebook group to market the library book club to potential participants as well.

How to Download and Register a Facebook Account

The free Facebook mobile application is available for download from major app stores like iTunes and Google Play. Each provider lists information on the app's ratings from users, specifications, and operating system compatibility for mobile devices.

1. Using a mobile device, search for Facebook in the app store.
2. After the app has downloaded, Facebook asks new users to Log In or Sign Up for Facebook. Select Sign Up for Facebook.
3. Facebook shares its immediate terms of services with new users before guiding them to click Get Started. The brief explanation says, "By signing up, you agree to our Facebook Terms [link provided] and that you have read our Privacy Policy [link provided], including our Cookie Use [link provided]. You may re-

ceive SMS Notifications from Facebook and can opt-out at any time." Click Get Started.

4. Facebook users may register for a Facebook account with an e-mail address or mobile phone number. Enter the appropriate contact information for the library's official Facebook account.
5. Create a password for the Facebook account.
6. Enter a birthdate for the account. Facebook requires registrants to be at least thirteen years old before they can create an account (in some jurisdictions, this age limit may be higher). Creating an account with false information or registering an account on the behalf on a user under the age of thirteen is a violation of Facebook terms of service.
7. Select a gender for the library Facebook account.
8. Give the appropriate password for the library's Facebook account to complete registration.

How to Create a Facebook Profile

After completing registration, Facebook tells its new users to "add a profile picture so friends can find you."

1. Select Choose a Photo to choose a photo from the mobile device being used to create the library's Facebook account. Select Take a Photo to take a photograph to use for the library's Facebook profile photo.
2. To see who is already on Facebook that is also connected to the library, upload contacts from the mobile device. Facebook allows users to select accounts to follow from their mobile device's list of contacts. This step can be skipped and returned to at a later date.
3. From information provided during registration, such as the new account's geography and account details, Facebook suggests friends to connect with through the library's Facebook profile. Tap the Add Friend button next to users' names to add them as friends.

   Customarily libraries follow other libraries in their service community as well as state and national library associations. Connecting to popular users and accounts in the community can help drive new friends (followers) to the library's Facebook page by piggybacking on their popularity and shared customer base. This step can be skipped and returned to at a later date.

4. Tap the More button on the bottom right corner of the library Facebook profile. The More button gives users access to update information on the account, search for friends, add events, and create pages and groups.

How to Create a Facebook Group

1. After clicking the More button in the account's profile, select Create Group beneath the Groups tab.
2. Name the group. TheMunicipalLib is naming the group after its existing book club name, "Reel Good Reads Book Club."
3. Choose the privacy setting for the library's Facebook group. The Public privacy setting allows anyone to see the group, its members, and their posts. The Closed privacy setting allows anyone to search and find the group but only permits members to see posts. The Secret privacy setting allows only members of the group to find and view posts. Creating a public library Facebook group increases the chances of discovery and allows the library's Facebook followers to learn about the Reel Good Reads Book Club.
4. Select Continue and add users to the group by searching their names. Facebook groups must include at least one member. Selecting other members of the library staff to join the Facebook group markets the Reel Good Reads Book Club on their personal Facebook page to their Facebook friends.
5. Tap Add a Cover Photo to add an image for the group. Unlike Facebook profiles or pages, Facebook groups do not have account avatars. TheMunicipalLib's logo of a movie reel flowing from an open book is used in the library's newsletter, press releases, and signage and will be added as the image for the library's Facebook group.

How to Post in a Facebook Group

Facebook groups allow users to post text, images and videos, and files. All media types have advantages to conducting a social media compo-

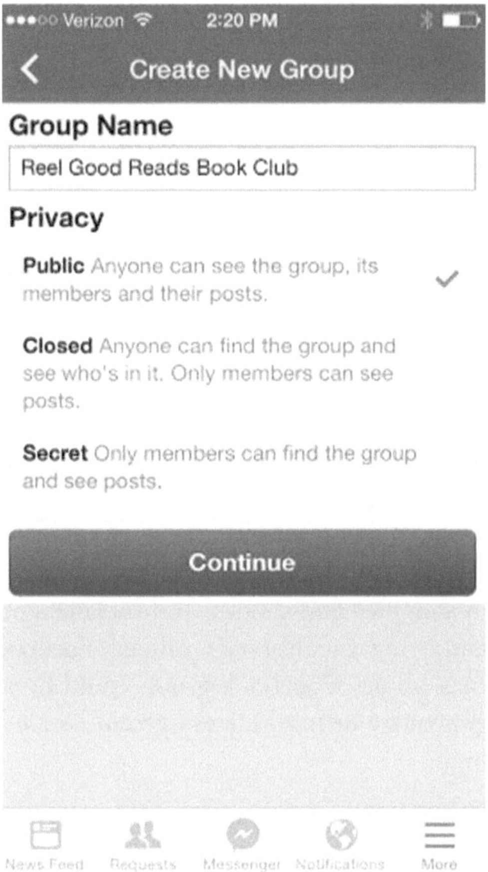

Figure 5.9. Creating a Facebook Group.

nent to a library book club. Posts should be engaging. User content should be strongly regulated. Added members should be considered carefully as they will have the potential to post directly on the library's Facebook group.

TheMunicipalLib's first post will be to invite users to learn more about the Reel Good Reads Book Club at the library.

1. Tap Write Post to create a text post.
2. Type a message. TheMunicipalLib's inaugural Facebook group post reads, "Check out the Reel Good Reads Book Club. We meet over lunch each Thursday at noon in Meeting Room A and

discuss popular fiction before its film adaptation releases into the theatre. Register to enjoy great conversation, tasty snacks, and the occasional book themed activity by calling the library or commenting below."

3. Select the camera icon at the bottom of the Write Post button to add a photo to the post if applicable. Select the plus sign icon to tag Facebook friends as applicable. Tap the location icon to add a geographic tag to the post.
4. Tap Post to share with the Facebook group and followers.

Remember to regularly check the status of the Facebook group posts and to develop a schedule of potential Facebook updates to the group during Reel Good Reads Book Club activities. A record of the book club's activity on Facebook allows library stakeholders and potential book club participants to learn about the group and what it has to offer the library's service community.

Future title selections to be read by the group, plans for Reel Good Reads Book Club activities and snacks, and socializing can occur in the group without cluttering the library's official Facebook page. Other considerations for a library Facebook group could be a Teen Advisory Board group, a genealogy or local history group, and even a Friends of the Library group.

6

TIPS AND TRICKS

Developing a mobile social marketing plan for a library requires considerable foresight, as previously discussed in chapter 2. There are key components to an effective mobile social marketing policy. Defining key demographics, establishing a team of staff, and organizing the necessary training and scheduling to maintain a pronounced social media presence should occur before the first post. Here are some additional best practices and tips for how best to utilize today's mobile social marketing applications.

Refer to the organization's policies and procedures that have relation to mobile social marketing policy. The library's approach to customer service as well as use of library records and conduct policies influence the voice and styling of a library's social media content and should be appraised during the planning process.

START SMALL

Most social media accounts are free with relatively simplistic steps of registration. Having a library account for every new social network is possible but not probable. Choose one of the large social media outlets—Facebook, Instagram, Snapchat, Twitter, Tumblr, or Vine—and create a tremendous marketing platform. When the time is right, the experience can be transferred to the next mobile social network presence. The objective of a strong mobile social marketing policy is to have a few strong accounts rather than subpar accounts for every possible network.

Before launching a significant social media campaign, begin with a plan to post regularly. Weekly events on staff picks or "Throwback Thursdays" on past library events and old library photos will establish the existence of the library as a consistent social media contributor.

All components of mobile social marketing should be examined and allocated to the appropriate resources and staff. Host a few brainstorming sessions with interested members of staff. Reach out to professional contacts that have experience with mobile social marketing to learn from their experience. Gather up all the fantastic and complex ideas for future campaigns. Jotting down easy wins as well as goals to aspire to creates a holistic survey of marketing possibilities.

Deem ways to be unique. How will the library's social media account differ from the community's other organizations? Evaluate the library's mobile social niche in its service community. Will the library offer public service announcements for school closings, weather reports, and community happenings on its page? Should the library focus on photos of its collection?

Review the social media posts from other libraries. How did they begin and by what methods did they gain followers? Apply their methods and extrapolate a rate of likes, interactions, and engagement that can be quantified and tracked. A good social marketing plan will have a clear vision of the next three months of activity. At all times, a quarter of a year's worth of scheduled posts or a calendar of potential posts should be handy to the social marketing team.

WHEN TO REINVENT THE WHEEL

Develop consistency through all mobile social media accounts by using the same or similar avatars, bio, and voice for social updates. Mobile social accounts typically provide options for color scheme, logo and backdrop images, and account name. All accounts should be clear to followers. When possible, a link back to the library site should be made available (typically in the bio line). Visitors to a mobile social network should not have to guess what the account represents.

Connecting mobile social media adds another level of uniformity while allowing content to be posted one time to multiple platforms. Librarians can save themselves the work of re-creating the same information for one event, program, or resource through synced social media accounts.

Seek library-related information that can be useful to link to on social media as well. There is little point in reinventing the wheel so to speak when other professionals have created content they are willing to share. Information about popular media, books adapted into films, and news connected to the fields of library science and information technology are fodder for social media posts. Link back to original posts from other libraries, news outlets, and content creators to establish a rapport and increase the connection between the marketing audience, social sources of information, and the library's social media. Integrate when possible. Eliminate repeatable work.

Energy and resources should be spent on developing a remarkable brand. A social media marketing team should reinvent the wheel when it comes to defining its brand and creating unique user experience through inventive advertising.

MAKE A CONNECTION

Relatable advertising is the strongest. Brands that demonstrate humor and storytelling that are reminiscent of the audience's life view produce the strongest meaning and reach. Telling the library's story through the eyes of its patrons is naturally going to be more engaging to its patrons. Posting updates that feature patrons show what the library can do on a personable level.

Share daily moments at the library, such as a user obtaining his or her first library card. Encourage users to talk about their first library card. Ask closed-ended questions. For example, "What is your favorite service accessible with your library card?" Close-ended questions help to keep social media followers moving in a direction that supports the message of the library's marketing.

Contests are another avenue of connection. Prompting participation with incentives can help boost a social media contest. If a library does not have a budget line in its marketing budget for incentives, its social marketing team could look to local businesses or even its Friends of the Library group to support promotion of services. However, the social media value of being acknowledged, "liked," and commented upon cannot be undervalued. Many library followers will remain loyal if the library's social media presence is active and responsive.

Humanize the brand by using consumer quotes as much as possible. When a patron writes a letter to the library or praises services to staff working at the desk, the opportunity should be taken to share the positive review as broadly as possible. Some library social marketing teams keep comment sheets at the library in order to collect and share the positive feedback on social media as well as the useful criticism to library management. As social organisms, people respond well to brand attempts to interact.

Reward followers for their social media attention. With permission, share photos and videos of patron activities on Instagram or Vine as they enjoy library services, programming, and events. Patron-focused marketing thanks users for their patronage and demonstrates how patrons take advantage of all that the library offers.

DEFINE THE BRAND

Defining the library's brand is the first step of its mobile social marketing. The process of defining a brand demands much research, assessment, and even a SWOT (strengths, weaknesses, opportunities, and threats) inventory. Characteristics of the library that give it an advantage as an educational, entertainment, and social hub in the community should be noted. Weaknesses in service or limited service placing the library at a disadvantage should be noted. Opportunities that can be exploited to the advantage of the library and its users should be noted. Circumstances that threaten the library's service model should be noted as well.

A mobile social marketing plan is guided by the brand's business philosophy, model statement, SWOT assessment, and service community statistics. Take inventory of staff skills and library resources to juxtapose next to customer needs in order to develop posts. After the cognitive phase of defining a brand is complete, the active phase is created by these practices:

- Gain insight into the community. Follow community social media accounts to learn what is being talked about. Jump into the conversation and document what is important and interesting to users.
- Build visibility. Make the brand known by integrating updates through popular accounts. Talk to local radio, newspaper, and media outlets about featuring the library's account as it takes its first steps into mobile social media marketing. Construct collaborative campaigns to demonstrate the library's authority among the service community's social networks.
- Influence stakeholders. A library's stockholders typically consist of a college or municipality, a Library Board and its staff, and the remaining members of the community who are eligible for library services. Word of mouth from these stakeholders should be influenced by the library's brand definition. Work with stakeholders to manifest the library's social marketing narrative. Ask stakeholders to share what drew them to the library and how the library supports their needs to create the community's story about library services.
- Drive traffic to services. The main purpose of mobile social networks used to be to drive traffic to the brand's website. Today, mobile social networks employ marketing to drive traffic to the brand's services. Link directly to databases, learning centers, and digital resources through social network updates. Mobile social platforms are shifting to the forefront of enviable real estate for content aggregates. Ergonomic accesses to e-books and online collections should be a pillar of a library's mobile social marketing.

DOS AND DON'TS

As explored in previous chapters, mobile social marketing is a delicate practice with decided dos and don'ts. Mobile social marketing teams can learn from the triumph and failure of other brands and their campaigns. A mobile social marketing plan cannot take every possible variable into account; however, contingencies should be anticipated and grouped with clarion directives.

Dos When Posting on the Behalf of a Library

1. Housekeeping. Posts should have full permissions, copyright, accuracy in content, proper grammar, and correct spelling.
2. Engagement. Interaction is the crux of mobile social networks. Users want to see active, responsive brand accounts. The library's mobile social accounts should be checked and posted to regularly.
3. Keep calm. Eventually an unfavorable post will make its way onto a library's wall. Don't feed into a social network disaster. Keep the mobile social marketing plan at hand, which should entail steps to face dissenting or provocative posts rationally. Arguing or ignoring customer feedback on social media feeds into the disaster and does not reflect a library's customer service goals.

Don'ts When Posting on the Behalf of a Library

1. Anonymity. A brand's voice should be intimate and clear to ascertain by its followers. A continual stream of event promotion must be broken up with interpersonal posts to retain an audience's attention.
2. Overwhelm. Don't overwhelm a library's mobile social marketing audience with the overuse of automated updates, spam-like frequency of posts, and too many hashtags. The general rule of thumb for a library is to post a minimum of twice a week and maximum of twice a day. The reception of posts and their incidence will be unearthed in the first few months of a mobile social network account's life.
3. Don't interpret the lack of likes, comments, or shares as failure. Each book left on the library shelves at the close of the day are not failures for checkout. To paraphrase Ranganathan, for each person a book and for each book a person who will eventually visit the library and check it out. The same principle applies to marketing posts. Some library posts will incite response; others will not. A library's mobile social marketing reach should be quantified and then considered along with its likes, comments, and shares about six months into its launch.

HOW TO TAKE ADVANTAGE OF MOBILE MEDIA FORMATS TO ENGAGE YOUR LIBRARY'S MOBILE SOCIAL AUDIENCE

Use photos, animated graphics, and videos as much as applicable to engage followers. Marketing approaches are increasingly tied with media formats that intrigue and inspire. If a photo can just as easily say what two or three lines of text can, determine a way to take a picture.

Graphic updates answer the demand of mobile social marketing dos and don'ts. A photograph or video meets housekeeping standards and removes anonymity. Mobile social networks make photo sharing simple and easily integrated to other platforms and wider audiences.

7

FUTURE TRENDS

Going forward with a library mobile social marketing plan, a librarian should occasionally check upcoming trends and keep an eye out for inventive marketing opportunities. Mobile social networks have changed the marketing game forever with their rapid-fire turnaround from viral to mainstream content. A funny video posted to YouTube on Monday can be used to sell a product before Friday if enough consumers feel engaged and continue to share the content around the world. The rippling effect of information grows exponentially for marketing purposes.

Tracking trends in mobile social marketing can help a marketing team assess their community's needs and produce fresh and exciting content. In the near future, the world of mobile social media will be influenced by user-driven content, natural advertising, mobile outreach, video, and wearable mobile technology. As the makeup of social media use changes, mobile social marketing needs to quickly adapt to users' interests and expectations.

USER-DRIVEN CONTENT

User-driven content will continue to grow as a standard of mobile social marketing. Vines are substituting traditional television commercials to sell chewing gum and Dunkin' Donuts. Instant sensations are created on social networks and then vetted to market products by major corporations. Companies like Virgin Mobile and Nissan organize contests for Vine users to apply their brands to create Vine advertising.

Since 2007, Doritos has held a Super Bowl commercial contest called "Crash the Super Bowl" for independent creators to compete for the most coveted commercial airtime of the year. Each year the marketing formula continues to appeal to the audience: consumer created, short, microbudgeted, and relatable.

NATURAL ADVERTISING

While native advertising (digital advertising connecting form and function on a mobile platform) is in its eminence, a softer, more organic form of native marketing called natural advertising will soon take its place. Native advertising takes the form of stratified responses for information pursued on a particular platform; examples of this would be Twitter's Promoted tweets and Google's search advertisements materializing alongside its results. With natural advertising, marketers course through followers' mobile social network activity to share information in an intuitive exchange. Native advertising is derived from macros in software and is a result of organic search and engagement.

Natural marketing has been incredibly favored when it addresses popular culture. In fact, the Shorty Awards, which honor the best of social media and recognize people and organizations producing content on Twitter, Facebook, Tumblr, YouTube, Instagram, Vine, and the rest of the social web, have a category specifically for Best Branded Real-Time Response to a Major Event or Cultural Phenomenon. A 2013 finalist for this award was PepsiCo for their thirty-second response to the "Harlem Shake by Baauer" dance meme that went viral in February. PepsiCo's responsive, low-cost rendition was among the nearly four thousand imitation videos created in the first two weeks of the viral phenomena.

Libraries are inlets for information flow throughout their communities and can easily adapt word-of-mouth, face-to-face marketing to their mobile component natural marketing. A follower's social update about music could be an opportunity to share some of the library's holdings in the genre as a response. However, a caveat to this approach is the potential for a misstep.

Mobile social marketing's rapid turnover as well as the very nature of natural advertising lends itself to social media marketing gaffes. In 2009, the official Twitter account for Habitat's UK outlet, @HabitatUK, found a bit of social media backlash for its use of trending tags to increase their reach. The marketing team's implementation of the tags #Mousavi and #Iran during the peak of Mir-Hossein Mousavi's presidential campaign were perceived as insensitive piggybacking on serious and contentious global events. Their tagging practice was abandoned after a social media storm unleashed upon the company throughout all major networks.

Mobile social marketing is a commitment to keep current to popular events as well as to evaluating an audience to gauge what is suitable, valuable information. Risks are inherent to discussion on an open forum and must be weighed against the benefits of engagement.

Public and academic libraries already apply their social media presence to respond in times of national joy and crisis. A mobile social marketing plan should delve beyond the federal holidays or cultural responses to liaise with the macrocosm or microcosm that is the library service community. Libraries marketing through their contributions to the natural communication of their users across mobile social networks can demonstrate the power of personal, natural dialogue.

MOBILE OUTREACH

Users will increasingly find their information through mobile means. In the early days of online social marketing, mobile social networks were an afterthought for new content. Today it is the first place they go. The future will bring progressive functionality of mobile technology for paying bills, scheduling appointments, navigating government resources, and socializing. As traffic moves from hard-copy forms of advertising and even away from the library's website, the mobile presence is the place for news to be.

The Pew Research Center found in 2014 that most Americans already own one or more devices with mobile access: 58 percent own a smartphone, 32 percent own some brand of e-reader, and 42 percent own a tablet. This level of mobile access makes social marketing on mobile networks essential for libraries to remain current and to reach the users directly linked to emerging library services. New library products and collections should be showcased to the library community through the immediacy of social network accounts. Users can be directed to the library's online catalog or website, give prompt feedback, and share the library's marketing with friends within minutes of a service being promoted through mobile means.

VIDEO

For the first time since its creation in 2005, YouTube has reported fewer video views than Facebook. The growing interaction with videos through social networks, applications, and mobile hotspots outside of YouTube transforms how a mobile social audience absorbs marketing. Brands must now use diverse, short-form video-sharing techniques through Vine, Snapchat, Instagram, and Tumblr to share their stories.

Anticipate increased integration of animated images, such as GIFs, by heavyweight social media networks like Facebook and Twitter. The popularity of videos and animated images have been explored by newer mobile social networks like Ello and Diaspora. Video production has become incredibly straightforward and inexpensive as well as a main feature for several mobile social networks. With autoplay capabilities such as Vine loops, the prevalence of video correspondence will continue to rise.

Libraries can draw from weekly events, the behind-the-scenes activities of library work, and so much more to record and share. Network integration makes sharing a video on multiple social media platforms uncomplicated. Observe how video and animation images are used for humor and responsive marketing as the use of this medium grows. Emulate successful campaigns and tap library users in the community to create a unique and meaningful library marketing experience.

WEARABLE TECHNOLOGY

Several industries are finding purpose and application for wearable technology. Consumers can track their exercise and dietary intake with Nike+ FuelBand, Fitbit, and Jawbone UP. These types of wellness devices have encountered a resurgence of popularity as the potential to share the information gathered on the device to mobile social networks has been added. Clearly a social media component to technology relates with its attraction.

Google Glass broke new ground and gave innovators an opportunity to learn how consumers react to wearable devices. While this project is closed, gauging how users adapt this technology to suit their needs has guided the steady stream of new wearable devices. Smartwatches place mobile social marketing around the wrist of an audience member and may tweak the way users engage through text, video, and audio media. For more on this exciting topic, see Tom Bruno's *Wearable Technology: Smart Watches to Google Glass for Libraries*, also in this series.

HOW TO LOOK OUT FOR WHAT'S NEXT

Subscribing to a few key news sources can enable a marketing team to stay up to date with daily or weekly summaries. While it may not be cogent to receive information on the minutiae of mobile development or tech-related legislation, a regular hand to the pulse of innovation will activate creative thinking. A few excellent resources are listed below:

- Ars Technica publishes news, reviews, and guides with a focus on software, user interface, and technology policy. To learn about the latest devices and how they will influence the access and aesthetics of mobile social marketing, refer to this resource for clear definitions and visual guidance.
- *Boing Boing* is a blog that began as a zine and then a website and finally a blog as it grew with available technology. This blog covers a gambit of topics related to mobile social marketing such as futurism, gadgetry, and intellectual property. Incidentally, much of the right of use and copyright information available on *Boing Boing* directly relates to the field of information technology as well.
- *BGR (Boy Genius Report)* is a specialized blog for mobile and technology news. *BGR* offers consumer tips for Apple and Android apps and products (particularly prerelease leaks of photos and specifications) as well as trending topics in regard to gaming and entertainment.

- *Engadget* is a web magazine with daily features for gadgets and consumer electronics. *Engadget* is a useful resource for assessing the broadening parameters of mobile social marketing and for libraries that assist with mobile device instruction at their library.
- Mashable focuses on social media and general influencing technology. As the name of the website suggests, Mashable provides the latest news on integrated technology and examines impacts to digital culture.
- TechCrunch is a news website that centers on start-up companies, emerging Internet products, and up-to-the-minute technology news. To learn more about how users engage with mobile tech and social media, subscribe to TechCrunch's feed or set its Twitter stream to give notifications of its updates.
- VentureBeat devotes a division of its website to mobile news. Its publishing goal is to offer context to help readers make educated decisions that can expedite mobile social marketing planning, which supports a library's investment into ongoing mobile tech education.

RECOMMENDED READING

Reviewing well-written books, articles, and active online resources is the first and most productive step to building a profound knowledge of mobile social marketing. Keep current by following writers, tech reporters, and librarians on their journeys into digital promotion of library content, collections, and resources. When possible, seek out opportunities to learn through webinars, workshops, and continuing education classes.

ARTICLES

Dankowski, Terra. "How Libraries Are Using Social Media." *American Libraries* 44, no. 5 (May 2013): 38–41. "How Libraries Are Using Social Media" details three mini case studies from the New York Public Library, Central Rappahannock Regional Library (Virginia) , and Multnomah County Library (Oregon). Three major mobile social networks are discussed: YouTube, Facebook, and Twitter. The principles by which these libraries found popularity apply to other social media platforms. Learn how to use social media to promote advocacy and glean statistics to support a library's mobile social marketing proposal.

Fichter, Darlene, and Jeff Wisniewski. "Content Marketing and Strategy for Libraries." *Online Searcher* 38, no. 6 (November/December 2014): 74–76. Darlene Fichter and Jeff Wisniewski discuss the need for authentic connection from content marketers. They expose librarianship's unique capacity for storytelling and explain how professionals can wield stories to market library collections and resources. Find methods to create content, assess approaches, and measure reach within their interpretation of mobile social library marketing strategy.

King, David Lee. "Social Media Teams." *Library Technology Reports* 51, no. 1 (January 2015): 22–25. David Lee King is a major contributor on social web, emerging trends, and libraries. His article covers the important steps of operating a successful social media campaign for the library including staffing, training, voice, and content. King's attention to assessing a social media channel's audience and methods to connect and engage are very useful to new social marketing teams grasping the identity of their service community and seeking avenues of communication. Keep current on social media trends, specifically as they relate to libraries, by following David online at http://www.davidleeking.com.

Nicholson, Heather. "Tips from the Trenches: Marketing in a Small Public Library." *Feliciter* 60, no. 3 (June 2014): 14–15. Heather Nicholson covers the strategic difficulty of offering a strong mobile social media presence and successful social marketing campaign with limited resources and staff. This article covers the free marketing avenues used by libraries of all sizes, such as a monthly community newsletter, free event listings in area newspapers, and mobile social media networks. Nicholson's tips for small-library marketing is an inspiration to large campaigns as well as to social marketing teams of one.

BOOKS

Koontz, Christie, and Lorri Mon. *Marketing and Social Media: A Guide for Libraries, Archives, and Museums.* Lanham, Md.: Rowman & Littlefield, 2014. This textbook is an excellent starting point for professionals working in libraries, archives, and museums. The systematic process of managing a social marketing campaign is disclosed. Informational guides include insight on the processes of SWOT analysis, defining the social media network's audience, create a long-range marketing plan, and creating mixed-media content to promote collections and services.

Martin, Chuck. *The Third Screen: Marketing to Your Customers in a World Gone Mobile.* Boston: Nicholas Brealey, 2014. The size and style of The Third Screen: Marketing to Your Customers in a World Gone Mobile will give library professionals a comprehensive handbook for planning mobile social marketing campaigns, developing meaningful interactions through various mobile social media formats, and enhancing library user-driven content and dialogue through mobile social marketing applications.

Peters, Thomas A., and Lori Bell. *The Handheld Library: Mobile Technology and the Librarian.* Santa Barbara, Calif.: Libraries Unlimited, 2013. The approach of The Handheld Library: Mobile Technology and the Librarian will examine the authority of atypical and typical library professionals. Case studies will reflect the innovative use of third-party applications that will assist readers to enhance, analyze, and promote their Snapchat, Instagram, and Vine accounts for mobile social marketing.

Solomon, Laura. *The Librarian's Nitty-Gritty Guide to Social Media.* Chicago: American Library Association, 2012. The timeliness of this book will permit library professionals to learn about newer mobile applications such as Snapchat, Instagram, and Vine as well as how to collaborate mobile social marketing efforts through Facebook, Twitter, Tumblr, and Google+ to create a uniform mobile social marketing platform.

ONLINE CONTENT

The Digital Shift. http://www.thedigitalshift.com. Accessed 19 November 2014. The Digital Shift is a daily updated aggregate of technology-related stories as well as features from *Library Journal* and *School Library Journal.* This resource is designed to help information science professionals to learn and offer instruction on digital innovation and tech that will transform the digital divide into a more equitable and manageable "digital shift."

Library Journal. http://lj.libraryjournal.com/. Accessed 19 November 2014. Melvil Dewey formed *Library Journal* as a trade publication for library professionals in 1876. Today, the publication is available online and includes information concerning library news, articles on professional practices, and academic book and library equipment reviews.

Mashable. http://www.mashable.com. Accessed 9 February 2015. Mashable provides up-to-the-moment news on digital innovation, social media, and technology. Its online archives hold a wealth of information on social network navigation and supportive third-party apps to improve mobile marketing. Mashable is where a library's audience finds the latest and greatest in gadgetry and information relating to a digital connected civilization.

University of Illinois at Urbana-Champaign. "Getting Started with Social Media: A Guide for Nonprofit Organizations and Government Agencies." http://uiuc.libguides.com/social-media-for-nonprofits. Last updated 14 March 2014. The University of Illinois at Urbana-Champaign has created an excellent LibGuide to assist professionals with mobile social media marketing. Tabs walk readers through strategy development, creation of a social media marketing policy, various social media tools, examples of library marketing campaigns, and methods to measure marketing reach and success.

INDEX

ABOUT THE AUTHOR

Samantha Helmick is a user experience and outreach pundit committed to libraries in their endeavors to adapt tech trends, facilitate resources, and invigorate staff who serve users where they exist throughout the community. Samantha is an author, editor, and international speaker. She received her master's degree in library and information science and master of community informatics from the University of Illinois at Urbana-Champaign. As a proud winner of the Iowa Library Association's Quality Time Award, she serves at the Burlington Public Library in Burlington, Iowa, as public relations manager and Twitter guru.

Samantha has worked with several library committees including as a YALSA membership chair, YALSA blogger, reviewer for the 2015 Stonewall Book Awards, LITA Distance Learning Interest Group chair, GLBTRT Committee and Task Force member, ALA Public Awareness Committee member, Collaborative Summer Reading Program speaker, and as founder of #ialibchat. Samantha enjoys attending comic book conventions and watching classic films in her spare time.

www.ingramcontent.com/pod-product-compliance
Ingram Content Group UK Ltd.
Pitfield, Milton Keynes, MK11 3LW, UK
UKHW012042150926
475560UK00001B/152

9 781442 243804